Home Water, Home Land
a prose poem

Katy E. Ellis

Tolsun Books
Flagstaff, Arizona

Home Water, Home Land

Copyright © 2022 by Katy E. Ellis. All rights reserved. Printed in the United States of America. First Edition.

For more information, contact Tolsun Books at info@tolsunbooks.com.

Edited by Percival Lind.
Cover art by Laura Thorne, www.laurathethorne.com.
Cover Design by David Pischke.

Set in Tenez and Mrs. Eaves.
Design by David Pischke.

No part of this book may be used or reproduced in any manner whatsoever without the prior written permission of the copyright holder except for brief quotations in critical articles or reviews.

ISBN 978-1-948800-53-2

Published by Tolsun Publishing, Inc., Flagstaff, Arizona.
www.tolsunbooks.com

for Qwynn

Chapter Water | to leave home

Crosses 2

La Pincoya 3

Up Island 4

Salt Scrubbed Heart 5

Roil 6

Subsistence 7

Whisper 8

La Petite Chat Gris 9

Clearcut 11

Volcano 12

Mingle 13

Hands 14

Out Crash 15

Shape of Gratitude 17

Afraid 18

Offerings 19

Just lines we cross, 20

Northward Course 21

Good as Home 22

Halfway 23

Pigeon Voyageur 24

New Skin 26

Mowita 27

Rock and Root 29

Want 30

Fend 31

Come Morning 32

Everything Remotely Useful 33

Mutable 34

Chapter Land | the growing season

to alight on a surface 36

solid part of the earth's surface 38

to come to the end of a course or to a stage in a journey 40

to touch at a place on shore 42

the people of a country: Lena 44

REALM, DOMAINE (shadow–) 46

COUNTRY 48

to catch and bring in 50

the people of a country: Krisitanne and Elysia 52

places where Bible stories happened (Holy–) 54

a rural area characterized by farming 56

GAIN, SECURE (–a job, –a leading role) 58

the surface of the earth and all its natural resources 60

REALM, DOMAINE (–of make-believe) 62

to bring to a specified condition 64

to complete successfully 67

REALM, DOMAINE (–of dreams) 69

the people of a country: Sandra 71

to come to be in a condition or situation 73

a corresponding part of a celestial body (such as the moon) 74

to cause to come to rest in a particular place (–a punch) 76

REALM, DOMAIN (never-never–) 78

the people of a country: Hilary, My Brother and Me 80

to go ashore from a ship: DISEMBARK 82

area of a partly machined surface left without machining 90

to strike or meet a surface (as after a fall) 92

a portion of the earth's solid surface distinguishable by
boundaries or ownership 94

to bring to a landing (a perfect–, crash–) 95

COUNTRY (mother–, father–) 97

ground or soil of a specified situation, nature, or quality 99

COUNTRY (home−) 111
to set down after conveying 113

Chapter Home | you and I became us

September 12th 116
Wake: Post− 117
Contort: Pre− 118
Enter: Post− 119
Join: Pre− 120
Escape: Post− 121
Suspend: Pre− 122
Circle: Post− 123
Witness: Pre− 124
Hold: Post− 125
Define: Pre− 126
Desert: Post− 127
Close: Pre− 128
Peer: Post− 129
Float: Pre− 130
Splinter: Post− 131
Reverberate: Pre− 132
Empty: Post− 133
Ignite: Pre− 134
Search: Post− 135
Mottle: Pre− 136
Face: Post− 137
Ring: Pre− 138
Prepare: Post− 139
Birth 140
Gaze: Post− 141
Spiral: Pre− 142
Notes
Gratitudes

Chapter Water
to leave home

Crosses

What once washed over me, comes again, and goes, like the grays and orcas, like tides and moons, the desired and detested, what gives way and got away. I escaped not only a country, but a childhood of spindly crosses to bear. Wishing rocks and uncracked geodes.

I crossed the Forty-Ninth Parallel

like a little girl hell-bat, surprised to be changed by nothing but a manmade border. My '63 Chevy Nova packed to the gills with essentials for university life in Canada. My slippery American heart already swimming upstream to a foreign land. I can still feel my hemispheres part. Feel North a rush of steelhead, South a sweep of sargassum mirrored in waves. Feel beneath Cedar River's gravel bend, a flush of roe.

La Pincoya

He sailed her–his wooden boat already christened with
the name *La Pincoya*–from Chile. This sailboat is not
where I live but I take to it like home. I live in Victoria,
the capital of British Columbia, five hours southwest
of Tofino, where he lives tied to the Crab Dock, a
government wharf a half mile from the village. He tells
me the myth of La Pincoya, the sea spirit:

> if she faces the sea
> when dancing the shore,
> then will come
> an abundance of fish;
>
> > her face
> > to the mountains
> > foretells
> > a season of loss.

He stokes the small woodstove with bits of driftwood
that momentarily resemble toy birds or rabbits while
portholes circle distant mountain trees–cathedral
groves where light grows scarce.

Up Island

We met off-season–gray whales not yet in full migration–in the kayak/coffee/book shop. Second-year final exams behind me, I drove my four-door Chevy Nova–a car seven years older than me–with its broken speedometer, up island on my first solo road trip. I slept on the back bench seat, read Michael Ondaatje's *Running in the Family* by flashlight in the parking lot at the trailhead for Green Point campground while rain pebbled the steel roof. Next morning, rain almost defeated me but instead of Victoria, I steered north to Tofino, where the highway ends, and the waterways of Clayoquot Sound begin. Where I–with him–began.

Salt-Scrubbed Heart

I migrate from Victoria to Tofino for four summers, like the grays that swim a yearly ribboned path from Baja, Mexico to Alaska's Bering Sea. Come April I leave the city behind and take root in *La Pincoya's* hull, a womb with the pulse of the ocean in her cypress keel, her small woodstove like a salt-scrubbed heart. Orca pods flash past. Gray whales surface, spy, and dive into underwater clouds of plankton, krill, small fish and crustaceans. Their tails, like primordial, mottled breast-plates, catch light and slowly sink.

Roil

Inside *La Pincoya* our berth fills the forepeak, meaning we sleep in a triangular nest inside the bow of the boat. Above our heads, a clear bulletproof dome attaches to a removable hatch. *La Pincoya*'s previous owner told the man that this dome once sat atop a Chilean army tank. Whether or not this is true, I chose to believe it. It's 1992, and below the Canadian border the L.A. Race Riots explode. They last six days. Fifty-six people are killed, two thousand injured.

Though I know my family and friends in Washington State are safe, I worry. Everywhere south of the Forty-Ninth Parallel roils with war of one kind or another: The War on Drugs. The War on Crime. Advertisements enact Wars Against Tooth Decay. These years in Canada I'm at war, too. I battle the reputation that clings to Americans outside our homeland.

I lie awake at night staring up through the bulletproof dome. *La Pincoya*'s mast and small spreader form the tree of Christ's cross. I want to pray for my family's safety, but my rote prayers wander, swoop and dive like schools of minnows directed by nothing tangible or sure.

Subsistence

His life changes according to the seasons. Spring and
summer bring tourists who pay him to take them out on
his whale watching boat to the bays and inlets where
the whales loll about before continuing north. *Leur
existence est notre subsistence*, I quip in broken French.
Their existence is our subsistence. (He asks if I mean
the whales or the tourists.)

I help him book tours out of the rinky-dink museum
housed on the ground floor of the two-story building he
owns.

Battered reprints of the village's First Nations people
next to laminated *Whales of the World* posters.

A whaling harpoon and small rusty cannon.
A scrimshawed sperm whale's tooth,
though sperm whales don't roam
this side of the continent.
Tight woven cedar baskets and mats.
A yellow yew-wood ceremonial mask,
eyes of inlaid abalone.

T-shirts, if you like, with the museum logo and phone
number to remember your tour, to tell others how to
find the place, tell others to come, see–

I'll never be good at sales.

Whisper

La Pincoya holds me like a grandmother and we talk of the past as I sand her teak brightwork. At times her voice drops away as if she forgot what she was about to say. Then I whisper to her how I want a child with the man, so we can raise a family on this little rocking home. Already, each month at the sight of red, the clench of cramps, I calculate the loss of what I've always wanted—a child. Something to set my life's course. I hear *La Pincoya* sigh in the light, a seagull's keer, a far-off buoy bell. I want her to keep speaking, but I'm still coming to understand that life on the water's surface is really a life below what's seen, an unsaid story expanding within the membrane of things.

La Petite Chat Grise

He, with his heavy Québécois accent, says, somewhere in the boat I'll find *la petite chat grise.* My hands reach into the kindling and paper box where she sleeps, our voices lost on her.

I never speak English to this little gray cat.
I never speak French to him.

How do I translate his gray-fur gift to me? A living thing meaning three of us now, meaning this is what he can give.

Should I reciprocate, offer him something that breathes? A hamster, a responsive indoor fern, or the child we occasionally whisper into creation.

I sing to her in French sometimes
> *La petite minou*
> *qui j'aime beaucoup*
using words with which he grew.
I rhyme and sway like a mother urging sleep.

In the evening, he returns and searches the wood box for the little gray cat. He wants to hold her tiny body, stroke her warm coat and padded feet.

I want to stand and say,

Elle est ici
she's here   and

What can we give each other?
What lives, untranslated, between us?

I want to stand but I can't because this small gray cat
has wound around herself and settled in my lap.

She's here, I say, my voice half lost in French,
the little gray cat between us.

Clearcut

Have I brought war north? Because newspapers in Canada call it the *War in the Woods*. But Friends of Clayoquot Sound, the local environmental organization, call it *peaceful protest*, or simply *Clayoquot Summer*. Every day for three months a crowd gathers to block the Kennedy River Bridge, which leads to untouched old growth forest. It's the bridge to a day's hard work or massive profits for some. For others, it's the bridge to sacred forest or unique biosphere research. When I'm not sheepishly booking whale watching trips or failing to sell t-shirts, I drive myself and whoever can fit in the Nova to the blockades. Or I drive to a gash of burned out clearcut along Highway 4. There, I pick up or drop off protestors living at Peace Camp–a charred stumpland locals always referred to as the Black Hole.

Volcano

I remember summer in the lower Cascades before the
volcano erupted and trees were green. Brothers, sisters,
cousins—we'd hit the woods unleashed like Pharaoh's
plague of frogs while aunts, uncles, parents tended the
cabin or, more so, the beer. Intoxicated under stars, we
breathed together around the fire.

At that age I knew only surfaces, our named lithosphere:
                          solid curves of Mount Rainier
        Goat Rocks
Mount Adams   St. Helens
                  the Tatoosh Range surrounded us
like a cardiograph's craggy record of an ancient pulse.

My family was united then. A shifting, molten love still
running underneath. Questions asleep deep in the silty
soil of my blind faith. We play with sparks knowing
how the Pastor frowns on us missing Sunday's Divine
Service.

Soon we will fill Folgers coffee tins with ash from Saint
Helen's gut. We will shake the evergreens in search of new
gray shades. I will be the one they excommunicate. My
backpack—heavy as petrified wood—will become part of
my body. And from lands of rainbow parrots and oceans
too turquoise to fathom, I will scrawl confused messages
on the backs of postcards home: *Wish I was there.*

Mingle

Robert F. Kennedy Jr. hits town. Midnight Oil plays a concert at the Black Hole. Ed Begley Jr. stays at the B&B where my friend works. A famous woman I've never heard of named Starhawk arrives on the scene. I drive several friends and protestors to a secluded beach on Kennedy Lake (known as Ha-ooke-min by the Tla-o-qui-aht and named by colonizers after Sir Arthur Kennedy, last governor of the colony of Vancouver Island) where rumor has it Starhawk will hold a spiral dance at sunset. We arrive to a bonfire that lights up a small stretch of sand as water quietly rattles the shoreline pebbles. Sage and patchouli. Smoke rises from snapping pine logs. The day's heat mingles in my hairline and under my arms.

Hands

One of the girls who rode in my car to Kennedy Lake takes easy hold of my right hand. A gray-haired woman takes my left. We join the outer ring of a concentric circle around the fire listening to Starhawk speak though I only hear every other word through the stand of people surrounding me. Nothing about me looks out of place here among the hippies and Wiccans and environmentalists but I'm a new girl pretending at womanhood. I try to act as if Hell exists only as a metaphor for life on Earth and not a real place to which I have been told I am one day bound. No one knows I don't belong here though they hold my hands, and we fold and weave and never tangle our spiral dance around the fire.

Out Crash

This is not church, but it feels like I'm praying with my whole body, my whole heart. Prayer is an act of worship and my father's church said not to partake in the Sin of Unionism or Syncretism—*professing Christians joining together in religious work and worship with those who are not one in faith or who are professing heathens*. The sweat of my hands mixes with the sweat of the women tugging me through the spiral, our voices braid into the voices around us, the rising smoke, the cool air through the limbs of the lakeside trees surrounding us. The mountains across the water like mute elders neither witness nor ignore us but their presence gives the spiral this fleeting living space.

Suddenly, the phantom satchel slung across my back
and filled with large, rough stones
breaks open.

Out crash the leaden rocks I carried
from my childhood church
across the border to Canada.

The largest—a geode that cocoons the moment I, a girl of nineteen, sat before the pastor and the church's men who told me that my questioning and denial of their Heavenly Father shall bring my swift destruction—rolls away like the door to an empty tomb.

I wonder:

> *Did I fall from grace or was I pushed?*
> *How to stand again?*
> *Are there as many people as there are paths to God?*

I let these questions wing over the lake into the evening. At this moment I have no way to carry them, no home to carry them to.

Shape of Gratitude

After the spiral dance we stand around the fire. We're told to close our eyes and when our inward gaze reveals it clearly, call out something we are thankful for. I see the shape of my gratitude:

La Pincoya's hull rocked by waves.
Wing kelp ribbons shush against her ribs.
Mowita–the name I gave our little gray cat.
Purr and fur and pre-dawn fog.
Tide floods the inlet.
Phosphorescence flows.

How to say these things aloud? The girl who rode with me and whom I barely know shouts my name. Heat rises to my cheeks, and though I know everyone's eyes are closed,

I feel too seen.

Afraid

Next day, I stand on the sidelines when men from MacMillan Bloedel, the logging company, read an injunction requiring protestors to stay off the logging road.

I stand on the sidelines when the RCMP begin to carry limp protestors away. The Raging Grannies. Greenpeacers. High school students from all over the province handing out woven friendship bracelets. Come evening I drive from the Black Hole to the Crab Dock where *La Pincoya* patiently waits, and I tell the man the things I witnessed. He warns me, as he always does, that getting arrested could jeopardize my student visa or lead to deportation. By the end of Clayoquot Summer, 12,000 people will have participated in these remote protests, 932 of whom will be arrested. Eventually, 860 people are prosecuted. Those prosecuted for criminal intent are found guilty.

I stood on the sidelines because I was afraid of being forced back to a country I call foreign. Afraid of a home that no longer knew me.

Offerings

From the payphone at Fourth Street Dock, I cry to my father, *We're saving the trees!* He sends me magazine articles and I send him clippings from the local paper. Our protests have made international headlines few can ignore.

My father once said he could understand why some people worship nature. I felt his forest reverence in the quiet of our hikes, how he presented us to the thousand-year-old patriarchs in their sacred grove as if to say, *Kids, meet the Holy Unknown. Holy Unknown, these are my children.*

My parents warmed our house by woodstove, so my father always prowled for downed trees, lumber scraps or unwanted, unused wood to keep us warm. *I could be happy stacking wood all day,* he said as we transformed a heaped truckload of maple into neat rows of firewood against our chainlink fence. He banked on this like he banked on my faith in his Savior.

I think of him–and home–whenever I split rounds, stack wedges, and hatchet the wedges to kindling we stow in *La Pincoya*'s woodbin. Stolen forest offerings we scramble-gather and save up for inevitable winter.

Just lines you made,

says Joe, our friend, a Nuu-chah-nulth whose ancestors storied this land into existence. We're drinking beer in *La Pincoya*'s open cockpit. Sunset. The man and I have moved to a slip at the very end of the last finger of Fourth Street Dock, more fraught with sauntering, camera-ridden sight seers than our old slip at the Crab Dock. After three summers I feel for the first time like a local, which seems to give me the right to be irritated by tourists–never mind they are the hands that feed me.

We're telling Joe, though he already knows, about the border between British Columbia and Washington State, how Point Roberts–the roughly five-square-mile southern tip of the Tsawwassan Peninsula on British Columbia's mainland–is the United States, yet Vancouver Island, which dips well below the Forty Ninth Parallel, is Canada. He shakes his head.

It took thirteen years to establish the water border around the San Juan Islands between Vancouver Island and the North American mainland. They call the Pig War on San Juan Island a bloodless battle because nobody–except a wandering pig shot on June 15, 1859–was lost during the territorial dispute that finally designated Haro Strait as the boundary, making all the San Juan Islands U.S. territory.

Just lines you made, says Joe. *We cross.*

Northward Course

People know *La Pincoya* by her octopus–bright green with flailing limbs and round blank eyes hand-painted on the white mainsail by the previous owner's girlfriend. Whenever we're out on the water, the townspeople wave or shout like pretend pirates, *Ahoy, La Pincoya!* A homeless home, she seems to belong everywhere and to everyone. To get here she sailed from Chile on waves like a liquid ladder. She heaved always forward without regard for the invisible rungs she climbed–the Tropic of Capricorn, the Equator, the Tropic of Cancer–on her northward course along the Pacific coast and into the Salish Sea.

Good as Home

Where you from again? Joe asks. He'd forgotten I was an American. When I tell him I grew up in Washington, just outside Seattle, he waves me off as if I'd mentioned the next village over, says his people are from Washington, too. He winks at me. *Don't worry*, he says. *In my books, you're as good as home.*

He says I'm as good as home and I feel a few shards of my calcified guilt for leaving home drop away,

stab the surface,

sink below, and leave

concentric traces of the daughter I was,

sleepless mother I caused.

Men's old laws

dissolve.

He says I'm as good as home and flinty splinters of my guilt, for not returning to the fold, smack to the ground at my feet. I pick them up, rub them together in my heart until they start a little fire like the lanterns that hung before people decided to build sturdy lighthouses defining the water's edge to sailors with nothing but a flame.

Halfway

Middle of my fourth summer in Clayoquot Sound,
we find a third new place to live. We decide we'll sail
up Lemmens Inlet and anchor in God's Pocket—in the
U-shaped curve of Meares Island—and commute to
town each day by skiff. Halfway up Lemmens, an old
engine-knock crescendos to an emphatic clank

                        and *La Pincoya*'s motor shaft breaks.
We tow her with the skiff as far as Adventure Cove,
where two hundred years earlier Captain Robert Gray,
an American merchant and fur trader, anchored his
ship, the *Columbia Redivia*. Here Captain Gray and
his men prepared for winter. In a matter of months,
they constructed a fortified outpost they named Fort
Defiance and a boat shed where the ship *Adventure* took
shape. We anchor and tie a line from *La Pincoya* to a
shoreline cedar, far from the pocket of our dreams.

Pigeon Voyageur

I learn French with him because I must have access to that tongue of his, transported from Quebec to me, an American (not as foreign as I'd like to be).

pouvoir - to be able, can, may, might
n'en pouvoir plus - to have had enough; to be tired out

His friends assume I know his language. He confesses *elle ne comprend pas*, tells them I'm American. My tongue, equated to loud tourists, suddenly not as foreign as it feels.

Radio Canada airs a children's program featuring lucid phrases: *Un oiseau qui porte une message.* And I perch, coffee in hand, ear close to speaker, following the pigeon, the voyager in his tongue.

I should practice French with a stranger so one day I will wake up next to him and say, *Nous pouvons, nous pouvons.* He wouldn't have to teach me. I wouldn't be seen learning.

There will be small pieces of neon green paper folded in triangles, hidden in the coffee tin. He will open them like wings and find my words in his tongue, carried all that way inside me.

Sometimes I circle above him, homing in on what it is about him I love or want to love. Over telephone wires, through café crowds, in the cobblestone cracks of medieval courtyards, I warble and coo, *Je n'en pouvoir plus.* I've had enough, I'm tired out.

But where to land?

New Skin

Not until I landed on Vancouver Island my first year of
university did I learn the Canadian name *arbutus* for
the tree whose rustpaper bark sheds in ragged swaths
from a sheen trunk. A tree like the one I grew up with in
my backyard and called *madrona*. We kept two rabbits
in a hutch next to our madrona in the wayback yard.

                       I'd gather the delicate bark,
look through it to the sun,
    cover my forearms in a
                 new skin,
                     watch it flit
to the ground–
       a strange snow.

In Canada, I was corrected when I pointed out a
madrona on the university campus. *Artbutus.* Still, I
peel that bark like a sunburn. Press my forehead to the
shiny flesh underneath.

Mowita

The man presented me the kitten after I'd broached the subject of starting a family, shockingly soon after we'd met. Golden-rimmed green eyes. Short, thick fur the color of heavy blue smoke. I baby Mowita with rich dinner scraps, constant cooing, and limit her resting places to 1) in my arms or 2) on my lap. I obsess over her health and well-being.

I stole her name from Anne Cameron's *Daughters of Copper Woman,* a book grown more powerful and useful to me than the weighty King James Bible the church men held so dear. Until I left home and country, I'd never questioned my birthright faith or the silent role of women in my family's church. Now I dared wonder: *Did Eve, the Bible's first woman, come from Adam's rib? Or was the first* man *named Snot Boy? And did he take shape from the tears and mucus of Copper Woman's lonely sorrow?*

Mowita was the first daughter of Copper Woman. She used pitch to waterproof her log house when Thunderbird's own Great Flood of sorrow rose. She knew she could safely open the pitch-sealed door of her floating home when Raven returned with hemlock in his beak, meaning nearby land.

Wherever my home is, Mowita is there. We curl together for long naps on my days off anchored in Adventure

Cove, the bulletproof dome removed, summer pouring over us. Near sunset, we watch the distance as the man appears. His small skiff wakes a broadening arrow aimed our direction.

Rock and Root

One day I row the dinghy to a small group of rocks no bigger than a gray whale's back that appear at low tide in the center of the cove. Mowita sniffs the air at the bow like a living figurehead. She has not set paw on solid ground for over a month, and zips from my arms onto the tiny island. She meows and paces, meows and paces as I row away.

Though it pains me, I ignore Mowita's cries across the water believing it's important for her to remember root and rock. She should learn independence, know her cat-nature, hunt mice or minnow. I'm teaching her to not rely too much on me. Isn't this what parents are supposed to do?

In less than an hour I row back to bring her home. I feel a shift between us, unless she has always held back, hid away, distrusted my too nearness.

You cross lines and things have different names:

Arbutus|Madrona
Fear|Love
Dove|Raven
Olive|Hemlock
Want|Need

Want

I'm a child who wants a child of my own. I'm young enough to be the man's child. When I was born, he'd graduated high school and was traveling North Africa, rolling hashish flat as paper and sending it home in an envelope to his parents' house in Quebec with a note on the back: *Ne Pas Ouvrir!* This man is old enough to be my father, though at a young age he was told by doctors that, due to a birth defect, he would most likely not be able to have children. When he finally explains this to me, I don't accept it. I tell him to believe in miracles. I'm an adult believing in childish hopes to defy medical science. And just below surface, I subscribe to the guilt-ridden logic that my past social and spiritual disobedience probably disqualifies me, and anyone I love, from miracles. He is unable to father a child and suddenly a child is all I want, is all I am.

Fend

Autumn arrives like a banshee in the night. We wake under our bulletproof dome to a cacophony of wind, sloshing water, the amplified hum of our wind-powered generator, and Mowita's deep yowls of distress.

Puffs of soot belch from seams in the stove pipe when wind blows down the chimney. The man springs from the bunk to check the anchor lines.

Even in our protected cove we aren't safe from this wind, shoving in gusts, tipping us sideways, threatening to drag *La Pincoya* to shore no matter the anchor's claw, no matter my whispered, fearful prayers.

Dressed in rubber coats, rain pants, and gum boots, we perch–one at the bow, one at the stern–with gaff hooks to fend our home from the craggy rocks where I abandoned Mowita last month. We're careful not to push too hard or we risk *La Pincoya's* hull dashed against shore stones, mast tangled in low branches.

Night passes this way: rain and wind bursts that ease off as quickly as they begin like the breath one exerts when blowing into globes of dandelion seeds, as if we are part of some Great One's unsaid wish.

Come morning

an opal sky flings rainbits against the wheelhouse and deck in rhythmless beats. All is calm except for the cyclone within the man as he surveys the lines and checks the shore for our small dinghy which came loose in the storm. Inside, *La Pincoya* is a wreck. The electrical system is down, including the bilge pump, and a thin layer of soot covers everything within the cabin. We gear up for town, pack as many of our belongings as we can. The man will find someone to tow *La Pincoya* back to Fourth Street Dock as soon as possible. Mowita squats and empties her bowels at my feet, her four legs shaking, her meows raspy with fatigue. I zip her into the front of my jacket where she curls like a baby in the soft, safe darkness next to my belly as we bounce and rear across the water's surface to an uncertain home.

Everything Remotely Useful

Lemmen's Inlet was first named Disappointment Inlet, I suppose because it's the waterway that leads to a dead end named God's Pocket–the paradise we planned as our summer home. Instead, we'd been stranded in what Captain Gray named Adventure Cove in the 1790s. He named the place after the ship *Adventure* which he had built on site within his Fort Defiance, which was also consructed then and there. Before he departed the cove, he ordered everything remotely useful to the indigenous people be destroyed. During the winter months, Gray had thwarted the Tla-o-qui-aht peoples' plans to attack the fort. As he and his crew sailed out to the open Pacific, Gray ordered a retaliatory attack on Opitsaht–the small native village which can be seen from the kayak/coffee/book shop window as you sip a cappuccino–leaving two hundred homes tattered and burned to rubble.

Mutable

I leave Tofino and Vancouver Island for the last time
with no anchor, no lines or knots holding me. The man
plans to spend his winter renovating a small apartment
behind the museum and in spring will prepare *La
Pincoya* to sell. Low on cash, I sell the Nova to a high
school senior in Tofino who treats the car like a
dragster and crashes it in a shallow ditch on prom night
somewhere near Nanaimo. The boy and his friends are
fine, but the old Nova is totaled and junked. I will spend
my winter with family, south of the Forty Ninth Parallel
where I will plan for a trip to Europe with a friend from
university.

She and I will buy open-ended tickets to London. We'll
look for work and travel for months

by sky and bus and

ride Eurorail through darkness

past ominous castles

and thawing spring fields   across

what feel like mutable borders,

arbitrary waterways

Chapter Land

the growing season

to alight on a surface

Daughter, I was like you are now. Held close. Certain of belonging. At some point, you may feel what I felt, what most growing girls feel when bodies and minds open: ignition. A spark that speaks to you of a life undefined by parents or church or school or friends-since-kindergarten that exists outside of your circle. Another circle, with a bigger circle around it. Terrifying. Enticing.

Your circle differs from mine, though. I've made sure of that. Tried to keep my definitions permeable for you. My belonging consisted of knots and tangles which grew tighter when I stretched outside to pull threads from hems, let fly the shreds of family quilt work. Honestly, I did not premeditate to unstitch my hand-me-down faith. It happened like a season change, like an unexpected flood in the normal course of the rainy season: a watershed.

But I've always prayed for deluge.
        Wet flicks, mist, drips, pelting drops.
Drum, sponge, fillfull, sog.

A watershed is not a place that stores water, like I always thought. It's a place where water is shed like fur or skin. Water–united in elevated communes of cloud and storm–wanders off upon hitting the earth. Water lands on a mountain's east face, and sheds east. West face, sheds west. Each drop sorted by chance and ridge. Unplanned yet momentous for the flow that follows, the direction fallen water must take.

I've told you how my childhood backyard flooded almost every year to form what we called Ellis Lake. At its deepest, where four alders grew, a girl could float and row her inflatable boat (with aluminum oars borrowed from the neighbor) in over a foot of rainwater. She could spin with the catkins, scan past branches that crack the sky, steer clear where grass blades stab air.

That was me, a few years younger than you are now. Little water strider alighting on a circle to myself.

solid part of the surface of the earth

On maps, islands look like puddles of land in a field of blue. Compared to the San Juan and Gulf Islands, Vancouver Island makes a giant splash. Largest island on the west coast of the Americas, Vancouver Island stretches almost three-hundred miles north to south, and sixty-two miles wide. The island's southern tip crowned with the province's capital city, Victoria.

I remember the café in Victoria my first night in the world among strangers who said they'd licked the pyramids forgetting the grit would clog their tongues, who confirmed Jim Morrison's head is missing from Père Lachaise cemetery, who basked on some island for months eating melons. I ordered black currant tea served in what looked like a test tube and spilled by a traveler's hand onto my open journal. That evening I wrote: W*here will I go?* in the pale tea stain.

I remember the curled strand of road to East Sooke where a trail parallels the shore, and headland rocks form a porthole where the ocean continues on the other side. A boy, my first love, pronounced *Ribes Sanguimeum* in my ear like a lapping rivulet, a name for black currant new against my neck. He guided me through the forest to showy pink, panicle flowers in spring, a mossbed made for deer. Two close strangers kissing cassis between our lips.

I remember dark moving water, cassis over ripe and thick purple, heavy berry cluster, my womb a nest of possibility, Canada's west coast caves, black-currant wine in a bottle I'd brought to bed one night, a man, someone I wanted more than ever to make me full, yet my eggs, seeds and berry skins spread against my thighs like preserves, spelled an empty name, a childless child, tide surged out, moon told wane, black currant body weathers desert sand, marble headstones, fantastic conceptions.

On maps these loves resemble lands at rest in my memory of wanting somewhere new to leave from, places I came to know like my own solid body on earth.

to come to the end of a course,
or to a stage in a journey

First time I sailed to Canada, I was your age. A church friend–your Aunt Hil–and I pretend-smoked real Marlboro Lights on the wide, sanded, varnished decks of the miniature luxury liner *Princess Marguerite*. Ship from another era, she held a grand staircase, a formal dining room, a cocktail lounge and, of course, a ballroom.

Summer.

Two unsupervised sixteen-year-old girls, salt air tangling our hair. We motored past Mutiny Bay, up Admiralty Inlet and into the maw of the Strait of Juan de Fuca. We floated in and out of ourselves, not knowing who we were or what the world was made of except what we'd been told: Good and Evil.

But we weren't either/or–with our New Wave volume up on the silver Sony cassette player. Sunglasses. Junk-food lunch. Strawberry Lip Smacker gloss. Barely contained laughter at an adult passerby.

We floated between lands.

Our ropes re-tethered five hours later in the Inner Harbor. For our safety and well-being, we were met by one of the responsible and smartly dressed members of the Victoria satellite congregation.

They were Lutherans of the same vein. They became my portal to Canada. Three years later, in September 1989–the same month the *Princess Marguerite* made her final voyage from Seattle, a course maintained for seventy-five years–I left home and country to become a university student. I would sail every route several times from country to country, mainland to island, from old and new.

Between selves.

to touch at a place on shore

When I say goodbye to my father
the lulling curves of earth
and pale green water sibilate deep
unseeable heaves of ocean
all blur
      and salt
  and islands shaped
like familiar animals
that tell familiar stories:
This bear turned into a man.
That raven's beak unsealed the clamshell
holding our world. Dark, unsayable
places never charted for me
on the full-color maps of the Holy Lands
in the appendix of my King James Bible.
Childhood hymns swell   crack   dissipate
      shoreline ions   pearl dust

> When she says goodbye to her father,
> they don't know the depth of it.
> They don't know goodbye
> means she will return as a girl who swapped
> Christ's cross and crown of thorns
> for apple seeds and snail shells.

> A girl who will open: arms   legs
> her question-making mouth.

The M.V. *Elwa* heaves her and her belongings
up San Juan Channel   across Haro Strait
until the planks of her faith
thud
against
Vancouver
Island's
coast-
line.

the people of a country: Lena

Lena welcomes me into her tall house. I rent an upper room where a Garry Oak's arms flex and flow parallel warped windowpanes. Outside this tree-room window, the neighborhood's a dark land crowded with outcropped boulders between prim stucco homes. Downstairs, under fluorescent kitchen lights, Lena chain smokes Du Mauriers, asks me to sit a spell and chat a bit before my bus to uni. Always there'll be one pint of light beer with pizza Friday nights. Always percolated coffee at rest on the stove. A daily sack lunch for me, daughter she always wanted.

Thirty-five years ago, believing herself barren, she'd convinced her husband, Cedric, to adopt a son. She became pregnant with a second almost simultaneously. Their third son tumbled down a cement window well as a toddler, never to fully recover. Cedric drinks at the Legion any chance he gets. In the gut of night, I hear him clunk through the front door, sizzling bacon, slurring curses.

Lena says Cedric gives up religion every time he watches his third boy jostle awkward down the stairs or drool at dinner. Even so, he permits Lena to host the Seattle pastor once a month in their home. She tells me she believes this is a sign that one day her husband will be saved, but she also suspects it's his way of showing off his handy work. On Pastor Sundays our pocket congregation gathers in the sitting room, a sanctuary Cedric designed and created with alternating panels of green marble and red velvet wallpaper, like a room in a castle on a plot of grass-tufted land.

REALM, DOMAIN
(shadow–)

Sundays without Pastor in Victoria, we hold Divine Service in a windowless funeral-home chapel on Yates Street. Someone presses PLAY. We stare at speakers screwed into the ceiling to the right and left of the place where caskets rest during memorials. After a jolt of organ music, Pastor's voice delivers Old Testament Law with a pinch of New Testament Gospel, the shoulds and should nots, and how watchful we must be–just like home–only here his voice sounds edged with tin. In my head I call this *funeral church*.

We're not allowed to use the chapel bathroom so before the sermon I slip out an unlit exit that opens into the garage where two polished hearses rest side by side like dark, stilled lungs. Each hearse faces a cremation oven built into a brick wall, which I ease past. The thick metal doors curve on top and bolt tight shut on the side. Beneath each oven door there's a small, flimsier metal door. I've seen animals move through similar sized doors, coming and going as they please into their human's house. The bathroom's small and crammed with mops and buckets, Windex, Bon Ami.

I ache for home. For our little church on Fontene Street, its congregation of sixty souls. For my family. My parents and grandparents. People of my country. In Seattle, my oldest brother is in charge of tape-recording Divine Service. From my pew in the dim funeral parlor, I strain to hear familiar voices belting out the old German hymns. The organ, helmed by the pastor's grown, pimpled son, whines and drones full bore. Was that my sister's soprano? Did my brother whisper hello? There! I recognize my grandfather clearing his throat with a rough stuttered grumble.

In Victoria we are seven women, five children, and two men. We have no live mouthpiece in our shadow church. No catechism-confirmed men. And women–confirmed or not–are forbidden to speak to congregations. I envision the anatomy of cassette tapes. Reels and heads and tape guides. On one reel a black circle grows larger. Next to it, the other circle shrinks away after having spun distant messages like eulogies for my life back home.

COUNTRY

First day of Psych 100 the professor invites students to call out words they associate with the people of two different countries:

Americans	Canadians
loud	polite
fat	aware
ignorant	funny
overly friendly	peaceful
self-centered	reserved
racist	travelers
obnoxious	intelligent
rich	open-minded
rude	
war mongers	

I scribble notes with my head down.

***

During a break in English Composition, a girl I've been chatting with in class who'd asked me where I'm from, washes her hands next to me in the bathroom and speaks to me through our reflections in the mirror. *I kind of thought you were American because you have such big teeth,* she says and follows with profuse apologies.

***

In Canada, like in every creative writing class I've ever taken or will take, we are told to separate the poet from the speaker in the poem, to not assume the poem autobiographical. For example, the classmate who continually writes about horses and his girlfriend's flanks, should not himself be assumed to own a horse or to ride women.

***

After CW 101, in the cafeteria where me and other creative writers from class share fries covered in brown gravy, I say or do something I always say or do in the way I've always said and done it. And the one who wrote the poem about her parents honeymooning in the Florida Keys says, *You can take the girl out of America, but you can't take the America out of the girl.*

I laugh too. I've never seen myself outside my borders. *We're sorry*, says the journalist required to take CW 101. *It's not* you *we hate, it's your country.*

to catch and bring in

Who was caught–me or him? I used to always wonder that.

The boy and I sparked right away. He was twenty-four and I was nineteen. He was as much a man as I was a woman, so when I speak of him now, I say he was just a boy.

Me, still a girl.

If I was *caught*, was I a lured victim, not responsible for my actions? This is what most people wanted to believe, but it was a mutual catch, like the burst and hungry journey of a fire that ends only when there is nothing left to burn.

The boy had sandy blond hair, eyes like green grapes in a bowl lit by the sun through a kitchen window. He was the sixth of ten children whose father was a religious fanatic who fancied himself a preacher. Overabundant corporeal punishment coupled with little to no loving touch set off inner anguish in the boy. In that family, any child's attempt to address their suffering marked them as weak and disobedient–qualities their father considered shameful, not Christian enough. As his children grew older, fist-ready, less pliable, the boy's father left his family and settled with a younger woman in a trailer park somewhere up island. He told me these things bit by bit as we held hands in the car parked atop Mount Tolmie or off Dallas Road. I felt entrusted with his pain. His history.

I was not baited, nor was I bait.

He was searching when he asked what I believed in, and why. At first, I liked being asked. He understood my love of poetry (he tried to love it too) and my desire to see new places. Only four years older than me, the boy had already backpacked Europe and hitchhiked California, while his older sisters stayed fixed on God in a Christian church. I'm not sure how they discovered the Seattle church, but they felt it most closely matched their beliefs. The boy had sworn off organized religion and God forever, but his sisters believed I could bring their brother in again.

And so, we caught each other.

the people of a country:
Kristianne and Elysia

His sisters introduced us. I could say it was their fault. I could say they had too much faith in my faith.

One of his sisters, Kristianne, married a Muslim (if she'd known our pastor at that time, he would have forbidden this). I met Khalid. My nineteen-year-old self thought he seemed pretty normal. He wasn't a believer, but I was too ignorant then to know anything about what he believed. Their house smelled like exotic spices and sweat. Sometimes I took their son Ali to the park. When I placed him in the baby swing, I didn't want him to think I was an invisible force behind him, so I smiled into his eyes as I pushed him away and he swung back to me. I liked to pretend he was my own. Without detail, Kristianne confessed it difficult being married to a Muslim, but she believed her faith would triumph over his someday.

Another sister, Elysia, married Jim, who was madly in love with her. She loved him, too, I could tell. (Like a girl loves her Christmas-present puppy.) He willingly–exuberantly!–took Catechism from Pastor to be a confirmed member of the congregation, which meant he could one day partake in Lord's Supper. As a man he would also become a Voting Member of the congregation, a privilege not bestowed on women in the church. Elysia and Jim exemplified the kind of coupledom I imagined for myself someday.

I wonder if the boy's sisters knew they started a fire the day they asked me to pick blackberries. My homesickness soothed by the sound of their youngest sisters and brother lively amid the thorns and ripe summer berries. How comforted I felt back at their home as we rolled out dough on the floured cloth.

The boy I would come to love sauntered down from his upstairs room munching apple slices. I couldn't believe my eyes–his eyes! Green agate shine. I'm not making this up: he slipped a wedge of apple into the filling. Later, when his sisters pulled our creation from the oven and served me a piece of blackberry pie–I bit into apple.

places where Bible stories happened
(Holy–)

I understand why people thought I could bring the boy back to God. When I picture myself back then–however faulty the image–I exuded Christian faith. I didn't need to go around testifying because I knew that *chief of sinners though I be, Jesus shed his blood for me.* I kept Him in my guilt-encrusted heart like a golden cup in a high school trophy case. And I clung to Him like a man overboard clutches a life ring. My ability to memorize large sections of Luther's Small Catechism exceeded my peers. When I visualized King James Bible verses broken on the page, laid out as poetic lines, I could easily remember and recite the passages with intonations that brought the words to life:

From a child thou hast known the Holy Scriptures
which are able to make thee wise unto salvation
through faith
which is in
Christ Jesus.

The geography of the Holy Lands thrilled me, especially because they were real places that still existed on earth. My grandmother, who taught Bible History to us teens too old for Sunday School but not yet confirmed, built Solomon's Temple in Jerusalem, cubit by cubit, vestibule, nave, and inner house. We walked the Exodus with her, scaling miles with our fingernails. Palestine in the Time of Christ, a colorful quilt of territories between the Great and Dead Seas, stuck like travel brochures in the back pages of my zip-up Bible. Though our church had no way to facilitate such a thing, I imagined being a missionary one day, like my aunt and uncle in Pakistan. How else would I see new and holy lands?

I was a Lutheran, too young to know if I was a Christian, but that's what I called myself. That's what I looked like. With three older siblings, I instinctively learned from their mistakes, flew under the radar so I didn't get caught though I did things for which I felt extreme guilt: lied about my whereabouts on Friday nights, climbed locked gates to fly with friends on park swings, occasionally sipped beer at gatherings no parents consented to having in their homes. I'd chew my nails to the bloody quick, then I'd vacuum or dust our living room—without being asked. I hated myself in the mirror. But to look at me, the world could see I was just bad enough to feel guilty enough to be good.

a rural area characterized by farming

The boy lives with his mother and four younger siblings in Metchosin, twelve miles west of Victoria, where farm and forest enfold, expand, and acquiesce to the rocky headlands along the great island's shores. We take long hikes in rugged East Sooke Park.

He wants us to buy land and make an organic farm, a home, a family together. I tell him I sometimes feel my brain is a prairie mazed with parallel ruts cut by the wooden wheels of countless pioneer wagons just like the TV Ingalls family breaking terrain under open blue sky. I want to tell him that sometimes at university I feel an underground heave push my mind's ruts flush with the surface or open an unexpected fissure. Other times I feel the ruts of my routines and beliefs deepen so that any new or divergent path feels impossible to forge. But he scoffs at my reference to Laura Ingalls Wilder, says pioneers decimated indigenous people, destroyed the grasslands with farming, and should not be praised in the slightest. He says Christian missionaries did the same thing all the while preaching love and good stewardship. I'm not equipped, nor am I inclined, to dispute these things.

What comes to mind are *backfires*. How Charles and Caroline Ingalls prepared for a distant, raging wildfire by digging a furrow around their log cabin. They set small fires outside this barrier to meet the bigger fire. With wet feed sacks they beat at the flames that leapt over the shallow ditch. Rabbits, birds, snakes, and prairie hens fled by the thousands. Flames surrounded the house until the larger fire swallowed the smaller and burned out.

I sense distant smoke, so I too dig a furrow. Late into the night, I comb Luther's Small Catechism in earnest, review doctrine I've become confused about, and arm myself with Bible verses that would directly refute the boy's arguments and support mine. I beg God for the right words to disperse the roily smoke of the boy's doubt which threatens to infect my lungs–

the flame of his hand on my thigh leaps up

–heat of his breath in that soft place behind my ear

radiates down my spine–furnace of his promises

warms every crevice of my body–fills the ruts of my mind

with a different kind of future–a new way of being–

a curious, passionate

backfire burn.

GAIN, SECURE
(–a job, –a leading role)

PASTOR/SHEPHERD
He wields the crook (The Book)–a poke, a prod, a pasture green, a question-shaped answer.

He knows each soul in his congregation better than they know themselves. Their lives are his livelihood, his reason to live, his grave concern.

He and his flock are a break-off from a break-off from a break-off from the Missouri Synod. What he lacks in numbers, he makes up for in fervent adherence to God's Word, which clearly states the pope is the Antichrist, women should not speak in the church, and we should not join together in religious works or worship with those not of our faith.

BOY/DEVIL
At first, it's not obvious because he says *I love you* without expecting a reply and his eyes mean it, but beneath his hay-gold fringe: the tender bud of horns.

He pretends he doesn't want to, doesn't need to go to university but he hungrily asks details of the day's classes when he picks up the girl in his ten-year-old rusty hatchback. He plans to be a self-made man by cunning alone, not student loans.

Some think he can be saved. Some think he's beyond saving. Some think everyone should be saved from him.

GIRL/LAMB
She's third generation flock.

She pursues the promising whiff of blackberries near the bluff's edge. Brambles snag her shaggy flank. Behind her, clusters of her soft fleece waver amid the thorns. She gasps–surprised to find her coat the deep gray shade of not-yet-set cement.

One day in the mirror, she'll towel dry the compass rose tattooed over her heart. She'll steer her memory over all the bodies of water she crossed alone.

the surface of the earth and all its natural resources

If left to my own devices, I would've worshipped trees. But I was always overpowered. In our wayback yard stood a hundred-foot-tall steel transmission tower we called the *power tower*. On an elementary school field trip, we hiked down to the hydroelectric plant at Snoqualmie Falls where gigantic turbines turn falling water to electricity. We learned how power travels for miles though watersheds, along overhead cables to light and heat our homes. A petroleum pipe ran underground beneath our backyard powerlines. Because of this, ours was an extra-large suburban lot, endowed with a heavenly assortment of trees arranged like so:

doug fir doug fir [power tower] doug fir doug fir
madrona & rabbits *(under the lines)*

---------------------petroleum pipeline---------------------

cottonwood   apple   corkscrew willow
(stunningly sour)

guest alpine   mountain ash   holly   ponderosa pine

italian plum   alder/alder/alder/alder   ponderosa pine
(sometimes Ellis Lake)

italian plum   dogwood   oak   ponderosa pine

lilac   flowering cherry plum   ponderosa pine
(petals that left everlasting patio & linoleum stains)

Ours were not like the trees we occasionally visited in the Tatoosh and Cascade ranges where my father's parents lived. No trunks big enough to hide inside or close-knit trees up to their ankles in salal and swordfern, but I knew my backyard trees like friends. My alders stood as elders without loom or awe. My hands around each familiar limb–higher and higher–in reciprocal hold.

For a time, we kept a pair of rabbits hutched under the lone madrona in the wayback. Chore and honor: I believed the bunnies loved me as much as they needed me. Every morning, all weather, I trudged across our generous suburban yard bearing fresh water and a handful of pellets to tumble into the rabbits' ceramic bowl. When rain hit the high-voltage cables suspended like party streamers from our steel-lattice power tower, a subtle hiss infused my ears like the sound of quick poured ginger ale. And fog hummed a low sizzle, vibrating moisture against our ever-hovering power lines.

REALM, DOMAIN
(–of make-believe)

People are less afraid of risks they think they control, and they're less afraid of risks that they understand, so the things that people are most afraid of are things they can't control and don't understand, and certainly power lines fall right in that category.
–Frontline: <u>Currents of Fear</u> Original Air Date: June 13, 1995

Our backyard power tower is the ruins of a futuristic cathedral under which we conduct innumerable groom-less weddings dressed in my great aunt's cast-off negligees the color of pencil erasers, our eyelids brushed with powder from gold moths' wings. We never risk imagining not marrying a boy someday.

Here the apples sting like Eden sings. The bee's sweet secret drone wakes the pit in our stomachs to bloom– boom-boom. The rainwater lake recedes to green plums now purple ripe as blades of grass in plenty. We are but khaki alder dust in the suburban wind.

A pearly afterlife all but guaranteed, we'll make it to Heaven because we live by faith–*the substance of things hoped for, the evidence of things not seen.* Our faith rests on many unseen and incomprehensible things like Father, Son, and Holy Ghost. A Triune God: three in one but not one in three. Pastor, from the tower of his pulpit in our small Lutheran church, shepherds us in our faith.

But remember, we are powerless. We cannot choose to believe. Our faith flickers dull to bright to dim to radiant–the Holy Ghost working belief into our hearts' corroded circuits. We ignore the needle buzz of overhead and inner currents telling us disbelief is not worth the risk of Hell.

One day we will meet a boy who will make a fine groom. The boy will not ask if we ever worried about overhead powerlines or underground petroleum pipes in our childhood backyard. He will not plant fear where there was no doubt.

Here we never fear cartoon signs depicting stickmen, back arched, chest attacked by lightning bolts. Eyes skyward, we're a gang of daredevil gawkers watching superhero neighbor kids scale the steel crossbeams up and up and up the tower's legs. And every Sunday Pastor leads us to see what cannot be seen with our eyes: the Devil roams this earth *seeking whom he may devour who resists steadfast in the faith*.

We power the Devil with the turbines of our fear.

to bring to a specified condition

You can't tell by looking at me, but I was born with Original Sin. That is, I was born *without righteousness, inclined only to evil and spiritually blind, dead and an enemy of God.* Yet I belong to the half of our species whose pronoun and gender rarely appears in the King James Bible, leaving me to now wonder just how much the Laws and Gospels apply to me (she/her).

Original Sin is both seed and condition. I picture it planted before my birth when from the womb I heard the murmured passages and reformation hymns my parents and grandparents somberly espoused. Our stern pastor watered the seed as he baptized me in the name

> of the Father   [*water   trickle*]
>   and of the Son   [*dribble   spill*]
>   and of the Holy Ghost [*a splash*]–

> three liquid holy handfuls,
> my fontanel bared at the baptismal font.

As I grew, my condition solidified around my baptismal seed and Original Sin either flourished or withered depending on how much I believed in the power of the Devil (he/him) versus the power of The Triune God: Father (he/him), Son (he/him) and Holy Ghost (they/

their?). Guilt became my second nature. Shame my gripping root. Forgiveness gave way again and again, for I was never perfect, not even at first breath.

I want to exhale my old definitions.

We did not baptize you as a baby. In this way, I ensured your first circle–the one containing you, me and your father–differed from mine. I do not concede that you were *shapen in iniquity* or that *in sin I did conceive you.*

I mean to breathe new.

Let me bring you to a clean page:

No one is born with Original Sin.

We forever sprout from Original Love.

That is not a seed but a ground, a holding place for all of us. Everyone and everything is held here, even if it sounds too good to be believed. We inherited a human nature poised for righteous justice. We are born inclined to kindness with spiritual sight, alive and friend to the fish of the sea, and the fowl of the air, and the cattle, and every creeping thing that creepeth upon the earth.

to complete successfully

My grandparents were mid-life Minnesotan transplants. My father's parents came west and settled in the mountains and forests next to Mount Rainier National Park. My mother's parents came west and settled in an unincorporated suburban neighborhood next to Seattle.

Both my grandfathers served in the army during World War II. My father's father kept his Purple Heart in a closed box inside the china cabinet near the woodstove that kept my grandparents warm in their simple A-frame cabin facing Butter Butte, or what we called Grandpa's Mountain.

My mother's parents not only became Founding Members of Saint– Lutheran, they *found* the church building itself. A plain, sturdy place. My thrifty grandfather replaced the sanctuary windows with panes of red and blue and yellow plexiglass. The altar held a brass cross, flanked by two brass vases that my grandmother filled each week with chrysanthemums, dahlias, lilacs, or holly from her yard. The pulpit stood like a jutting headland overlooking a mindless crash of waves below. And, perhaps most importantly, there were oak pews (six on one side of the aisle and ten on the other) like an honest-to-goodness protestant church anywhere. Without my grandparents' financial help, Pastor's small, orthodox Lutheran congregation would have long rented the shabby community hall, unfolding and folding metal chairs in rows each week.

Every Sunday, my parents, my brothers, sisters, aunt, and cousin sat behind my grandparents, who claimed the first pew. Behind us gathered the handful of members who either broke with Pastor from the Missouri Synod or who tried our services for a week or so. Members trickled in, trickled away. Upright and attentive in the first pew, my mother's mother and my mother's father never looked back.

Obedient and restless in the second row, I looked forward to the mountains.

REALM, DOMAIN
(–of dreams)

return me
  to the mountain's shadow dreamlands
where the trees of our untamed minds
  woke us to impossibly captured toads
     and moss-encased waterfalls

we skipped church
  for the mountains for my father's mother
and my father's father   no less god-fearing
  they neighbored the place where a river's fork
staved off ancient forest fires
  preserving the grove of the patriarchs

   [oh, i've lost count of my fathers!]

we stretch arms wide to hug a human chain around trunks
  hemlock western red cedar
unless we grow faster than the patriarchs' concentric rings
  there will not be enough holding-hands to go around

next week pastor will rebuke us from the pulpit:
do not forsake the assembling of ourselves together

   [it was not a dream: he made eye contact]

we should have bravely countered:
for where two or three are gathered together in My Name
                    there am I in the midst of them
for there is no malice in the mist of this,
our falling forest water
                    –only veneration

before i lay me down to sleep i beg *return me*
        to the never said
            and needed saying
        to the mountain's light

the people of a country: Sandra

Sandra knows Victoria's waterways. She invites me to Fisherman's Wharf, where she lives on a boat more motorhome than motor vessel. With red hair, freckles, and near-translucent eyelashes, she's the pinkest girl I've ever met. The strongest. She gives herself insulin shots in the thigh straight through her jeans. She's in my poetry class but plans to be an investigative journalist. When I tell her about the boy, about the fire between us, she invites me to stay the night as a cover to meet him later at his new apartment on Gorge Road.

She's the first to tell me the moon's gravitational pull affects a woman's menstrual cycle and that women, living together, synchronize to one another's cycle, at least that's what she's heard and will research for her mid-term article due next week. And did I know that Christians follow a pagan calendar by celebrating Easter the Sunday following the first full moon of Spring Equinox?

I add these things to all I don't know about my body and my church and I wonder: *Is Sandra the devil, pink with disguise?*

Night. Few Stars. Moon, a thick claw.

We plough the chop, hugging the waterfront in Sandra's

fiberglass skiff. She navigates within a few feet of an empty tanker docked at Ogden Point. The contrast between our tiny boat and the gargantuan tanker sets my heart pounding. Unweighted, the tanker's hull line rests well above surface level. The bulbous bow curves out of the harbor water like a jutting pregnant belly we reach   out   to

                                   touch!

In darkness, I scramble onto a rocky shoreline on the grounds of the boy's apartment complex. Sandra cups her hands around her mouth and enunciates over the gurgling motor, *Be safe. Don't get knocked up.* And before I can muscle over the rocks and weeds back into her boat, she's left an upside-down V in the water, deserting me in the opening.

to come to be in a condition or situation

My aunt had an accident and named him after my grandfather.

We weren't told who caused my aunt's accident. Husbandless, she raised my cousin with help from my grandparents and my family, my mother being her sister. Her accidental condition became public when Pastor read my aunt's Letter of Apology to the entire congregation following Divine Service. I was eleven years old, thrilled at the prospect of a new baby in the family, dismayed at the warped grief-face my grandfather wore. His shoulders sagged as if weighted by invisible gargoyles as he stood in the church foyer and shook no man's hand.

a corresponding part of a celestial body
(such as the moon)

The boy and I live on a planet resembling Earth.
We sleep curled in the light of our world's moon.
He knew my body before me.
I thought my body was for accidents (intentional or otherwise).
To be filled with someone's greater purpose.
A meant-for-me mishap to cradle and nurse.
With him I've become more body than before.
Even my words and deeds are my body.
Messages back and forth.
On my way to French class
I sign the No Tampon Tax petition.
Imagine the protest! Imagine a *bleed-in*!
Before now I never knew my blood cost extra.
I wasn't taught to *do the math*.
Unless you count colorful Sunday coupon inserts.
I felt I'd paid too much. But I didn't feel like thinking.
Nor did I think to feel. Parts and places. Of me.
He doesn't think. He knows how to feel my body. His body.
Together in ways I cannot settle my mind into.
Who creates my mind ruts? Forging. Furrow.
During *it*, I wince to think: *He ruts*.
Against a body resembling me.
This is the season my mind outgrows my sheep's clothing.
On a planet where Lamb and Wolf play each other.
I discover the body in which I live.

Under a waxing moon, half-rhyming womb.
One tide informs
the other.

to cause to come to rest in a particular place
(–a punch)

You are here. It astounds me almost every day that I'm your mother. Not an accident: a decision followed by hope. After years as a couple, and after months of traveling together, your father and I toasted each other in Galway, Ireland, declaring one another married by heart. You were conceived in that land. I'm sorry. Must be weird, your mother telling you that.

After my first time, I felt extinguished. Early next morning, I asked the boy to let me out a few blocks from Lena's house on Savannah Street. Found a leafless, sturdy maple in front of a stranger's house, sat on the dewy grass with my back against the tree and looked past the empty limbs at white winter sky. Closed my eyes and saw a spent bonfire: tarnished aluminum cans, blackened driftwood, ash, and soot.

It has become less embarrassing to talk with you about the three-letter word that starts with *s* and ends with *x*. Education has changed. You, at age fifteen, know more about how your body works–how your mind, emotions and hormones interact–than I did even in my late twenties. I didn't have family life and sexual health–or FLASH–like you've had several times already in school. I had Sex Ed. My gut-wrenching shock, embarrassment, and ignorance coalesced into complete denial of the facts presented to me in Miss Cowan's fifth grade classroom. I separated facts from my body. No questions asked.

Did I teach myself better not ask, or was I taught? Either way, I was not prepared for sex. I was not prepared to feel my body connected to him but disconnected from myself. As if my body could never be unshared and belong only to me again. I was not prepared to resent the boy for what I gave him. Nor did I expect I'd want to give him more.

After my first time, I felt sucker punched. Invisible medicine ball lodged in my torso. Didn't feel cold, but I shivered under that early morning maple tree. Manure scent of winter mulch up my nose. In my ears the thud flood of break loose blood.

Again, I'm sorry. I know it's weird, your mother telling you this. What I mean to say is, I don't believe it will be this way for you. I have to believe you'll land in a different place, because you already come from somewhere else.

REALM, DOMAIN
(never-never–)

For I will consider a wordless prayer.
For the lake is home to swans and named Swan Lake.
For it rests on the other side of twisty Saanich Road.
For this craggy island once tilled by ancient ice.
For half-buried boulders big as hot air balloons encroach
   the park I short-cut to the lake.
For I've taken to keeping apple seeds and jostle a collection
   in my coat pocket.
For like many girls in many places, I've been warned not to
   walk alone where man-sized rocks hunch everywhere
   like homes for hidden demons.
For memories uncovered by psychologists in the 1980s.
For when *Michelle Remembers*, the world accuses families
   and daycare owners of chopping up babies–satanic
   rituals in basements and famous cemeteries.
For saying doesn't make it so.
For praying doesn't make it so.
For I live by prayer.
For I circle Swan Lake using wordfull prayers to pray for
   words that are not my own.
For I'm plagued with questions I've never asked before.
For which men choose which books for me to live by?
For I want to keep believing not-my-own words that they
   make others believe the Word of God as I believe I do.
For *no man can be saved by another man's faith.*
For maybe a woman then can save?

For what do I feel bad enough to beg forgiveness?
For I want to go to heaven when I die.
For are these my doubts or someone else's–planted by
    the Devil in the form of the boy I love?
For *we love Him because He first loved us.*
For the boy loves me so I love him back.
For my prayers disintegrate to letters.
For I stumble the lake's mudstuck edge singing the alphabet.
For I am a spell caster, spelling nothing.
For I toss apple seeds recklessly over my shoulders
    like pinches of salt in a sacrilegious
    jumble of superstitions.
For my compost prayer of pips and dandelion fluff.
For my rhythmless alphabet drum.
For it is dusk and the swans gather somewhere near to roost.
For seeds in nearly all my pockets.
For I once lived in a land where twenty-six letters arrange
    themselves mid-air and settle as the perfect
    words to sow saving faith.

the people of a country:
Hilary, My Brother, and Me

We were two: Hil and me. Us in ratty, secondhand sweaters, pin-leg jeans, and purple-frosted eyeshadow. Us with our not-too-teased hair. We shared bangles, tapes, and missives written during the school week in spiral notebooks we swapped at church. Her grandfather was a Holocaust denier whose book on the subject was published somewhere, but we never talked about that. New to our church, she and her family grew the congregation by a handful of adults and a few children. I'd never loved a friend so deeply. I could make her laugh Sprite out of her nose. She promised to quit smoking, quit smoking, quit smoking. We were Christians. We wanted to be good. Us like branches from an unpruned, teenaged tree–fused in our reach for the same light.

**

We were two: my oldest brother and me. He took the breakup hard (his Catholic girlfriend wouldn't convert) so I stepped in. An unlikely pair, him being eight years older and me still in high school. But I followed his lead, his stoic love, my burgeoning love for him, his music: the Clash, the Police, the Fixx, Bob Marley. I learned our city from my brother. Saturdays roamed Pike Place, Tower Records, Broadway. Grassy views of unknown bands at the Mural Amphitheatre. He stashed a machete under the driver's seat just in case, and I felt safe with him. My brother. A man.

***

We became three: my brother, Hilary, and me. I begged my brother as Hil begged me to let her join us on our trips downtown and to sparsely crowded Mariners games. It pained me to see, week after week, how much Hilary annoyed my brother and how she longed to fit with us. Eventually, the seasons breathed us three together. Rainy car camping at Deception Pass. Double features and double wool sweaters at the unheated Renton Roxy. Through all these things, we didn't say it aloud, but our church was us—we were our church. I felt we'd fashioned a trio to withstand the evils of the world.

*

They are two: Hilary and my brother. At first, I didn't recognize their ignition, or maybe I did. In the strangeness of it I sought to welcome their union, thinking I would keep them both like the misrepresentation of our blood-pumping, human muscle as a Valentine heart: zig-zag cut down the middle easily puzzled together as one.

I stood as Maid of Honor in their wedding the same year I was excommunicated from our church.

to go ashore from a ship: DISEMBARK

My excommunication was a journey in many ships. The vessel *doubt*. The vessels *question* and *wonder* and *fear*. The vessel *love*. I hunkered starboard and port side in these ships' cabins staring out wide windows over khaki-colored, often white-capped water while studying for my Linguistics, Art History, or Computer Science exams. Ordered a beer because I could. Tater tots or poutine. Hours in landless limbo. Canada and the United States became a dream of the other, a memory or herald of me. I went ashore, but never felt I'd disembarked.

DIS–
1a: do the opposite of
    One Sunday I do not attend funeral church.

–EMBARK
Instead, I meet the boy in a cafe where we sip peppermint tea which tastes like freedom cool and hot down my throat. He talks about our children, how they would be *so fucking cute*. I feel my face ember. For the first time I allow myself to wonder what it would be like to *not* have children.

DIS–

b: deprive of (a specified quality, rank, or object)

I avoid Lord's Supper knowing I'd be refused Christ's body and blood at the altar. For fear I'd take communion to my damnation.

–EMBARK

One Friday night, the boy insists on treating me to the expensive French restaurant on Government Street. We know immediately we don't belong, but the boy pushes on. The waiter lilts how the escargot are purged, killed, removed from their shells, gently sautéed in garlic butter and white wine before being returned to their shells. *Their homes*, I think, as the boy twists a meaty morsel from a glossy spiral shell using a doll-size, two-pronged fork. Take eat, he doesn't say, and lifts the body to my lips.

DIS–

c. expel or exclude from

I'm home with my parents the summer following my first year of university. The boy's making good money fishing the Charlottes on his uncle's trawler. Unlike me, the boy is accustomed to swells and tides. He lets God fill and abandon him the way he fills and abandons me with his search for a God truer than Jesus. One day I receive a formal letter via U.S. post to meet with *my brethren* on a Sunday afternoon in July. My father is not a leader, but

I follow him to the meeting because he asks me to.

Our church basement swelters in summer. Windows won't open wide. The men find warnings in Bible passages they share with me in earnest. Hilary's father tells of his sinful hippy days when he didn't know better, reminds me how blessed I am to have been raised in the church. How I should know better. One of the pastor's sons–the one with kind eyes whose heart lives on his sleeve–regrets telling me the love I feel is not love, it's blindness, the boy's love is fleeting.

But what about their love for me?

Most of these men have known me my whole life. We've gathered for Divine Service every week and every holiday. Pastor made me laugh with deadpan humor and jovial renditions of *Sie Leben Hoch!* I love him. I committed my Catechism to heart and aimed to please by showing love and proper fear in the form of silent listening, post-potluck clean-up, and never swearing.

Their love is tough. Like a fist-size leather pouch that can only hold so many coins.

Pastor asks someone to hand me their Bible, tells me to look up Corinthians II 6: 14-15 and read aloud the plainness of God's words. My voice garbles with tears: *Be ye not unequally yoked together with unbelievers: for*

what fellowship hath righteousness with unrighteousness?
And what communion hath light with darkness? And what
concord hath Christ with Belial? or what part hath he that
believeth with an infidel?

–EMBARK

They ask if I deny Jesus Christ as my Savior. A single
word breaks the hours-long trance and expels me like
a slipway launches a new-named ship with a bottle
cracked against her hull. I'm a young woman in love and
in doubt for the first time, so the word does not come
from the holding ground in my heart.

The word is a seed I spit from my tongue.

Yes.

The men see me sit up straight like a weight shifted,
a low-tide stone lifted, a saltwater world enlivened by
light. My eyes instantly dry and bright.

Now, says Pastor, *your tears should start.*

DIS–

2: not
I've discovered *Knots*:

there is something the matter with [her]
because [she] thinks
there is something the matter with us
for trying to help [her] see
there must be something the matter with [her]
to think there is something the matter with us
for trying to help [her] see that
we are helping [her]
to see that
we are not persecuting [her]
[etc.]

–EMBARK

Because I'm taking Psychology 101 and Creative Writing 100A it's not surprising I discover psychiatrist R.D. Laing's book of imageless poems with its only metaphor the book's title: *Knots*. The poems are exoskeletons over which I drape my experiences and fasten my new body inside to see what fits.

Years later, I learn that R.D. Laing, world-renown psychiatrist who blamed parents for the psychological problems of their offspring, was an absent or treacherous father and husband. This is not the first or last time I will learn that a beloved male role model is not who he seems to be; that he means *do as I say, not as I do*; that he believes the rules do not apply to him. Who created these men of nots? Who will next unravel?

DIS–
3: completely
My parents could've kicked me out of the house, cut me
out of their lives as Pastor advised. As many churches
demand. As my oldest brother advocated and others
considered. Instead, my parents told me on more than
one occasion, *we will never close our door to you.*

–EMBARK
To this day, I'm unsure the date I officially disembarked
the church to dwell in the land of the excommunicated.
No other letters from the church arrived for me at my
parents' home. Maybe Pastor announced my status to
the congregation after Divine Service, like he did my
aunt's unwed pregnancy.

For a few years after that hot July day, I sometimes felt
moved to attend church. Of course, those occasions
felt grotesquely strained, staged, and hypocritical on
everyone's part. Those days I often dreamed of standing
in the foliage, tapping the crimson plexiglass windows
next to my family's usual pew. Dreamed of punching
through to the sanctum to burst forth a deafening
repentance–anything to be seen again. To be heard.

Though my parents never closed their door to me, I
mostly stayed away. Made a life for myself on Vancouver
Island during the rest of my time at UVic, travelled many
months over many years through Europe and Central

America. Now I have my own family, my own home on an island just far enough away from where I grew up. But for as long as they live, I will cross the threshold of my parents' door, the three of us tying and untying the tangled, barnacle-encrusted lines that hold us to one another's shores.

DIS–
4: [by folk etymology]: DYS-: disfunction
It's not the boy's fault he is damaged. It's not my fault the boy damages parts of me.

–EMBARK
In the sleepcore of night, I wake to discover the boy on top of and inside me. This happens more than once. We don't talk about it. Maybe I dreamed it.

The boy owns every self-help book by John Bradshaw and Louise Hay. I, too, devour these books. We want to be on the exact same page. In *You Can Heal Your Life* I discover that *Breathtaking antagonism. Mental eruptions.* are the cause of the scaly eczema on my neck, arm, and upper lip, but no matter how much I repeat *Harmony and Peace, Love and Joy surround me and indwell me. I'm safe and secure.* I itch and scratch, ugh so awful, ugly, red. The boy says I don't love myself enough to heal.

I take the boy to mean I don't love *him* enough to heal,

to be beautiful for him–because, like the moon, the boy's attraction and desire for me waxes and wanes. He believes in being *brutally honest* about how he feels at any given moment. I let him shape me with his honesty. I stop getting perms, wearing make-up, eating meat, believing a man-made religion is going to save me. It's not the boy's fault I make him my life raft.

DIS–
5: opposite or absence of
Akin to dismember: to cut off the limbs of [a person or animal]; to partition or divide up; remove a member.
Akin to dis-remember: to remember and forget parts.

–EMBARK
I am a member remembered as absent. Nearly three decades later, while helping decorate the Christmas tree in my parents' assisted living apartment, I find an embroidered ornament dated 1989 and thoughtlessly say aloud, *That was the year I started school in Victoria.* And my father says, *Yes. You left and you never came back.*

area of partly machined surface
left without machining

The girl sings Colourfield's song like she wrote it herself. *Whenever we kiss I get to feeling like this, I get to wishin' there were two of you...* The boy says it drives him wild. He calls it sexy. She hates that word, and this is the first time she hears someone use it in real life. *It feels so nice I want your arms to wrap around me twice.* Sometimes she pretends to sing absentmindedly, powerless against the song stuck in her head. *I love you so much I wish that there was more of you to touch* while out the car window Victoria's cityscape transforms to Metchosin's forestland. She fears and loves sexy, keeps it hidden under layers of flannel and Cowichan wool.

In the fog-ridden beach parking lot, car still ticking, he says if she keeps singing that song, he's going to pounce on her.

I can't get enough of you baby
Baby yes it's true

When he does–his chest a sudden wall over the gearshift, his eyes in her eyes–she plays at defending herself. The one fingernail she hasn't gnawed to a stub, just jagged enough to nick his cheekbone, and draw blood. He recoils into the driver's seat.

The girl can't speak, can't think how to tend to this mistake as the boy curses, studies the wound in the rearview mirror. She feels the nail on her right ring finger and raises it to her mouth. Salt. His salt. She gnaws halfway down the side so that when she tears it from the nail bed her own ruby saltiness washes his away.

A week later, the boy's doctor prescribes antibiotics and says he's rarely seen such an aggressive fester. The boy frowns accusingly when he tells her this, suggests she wash her hands more frequently. She chews to the quick, pulls her thick sweater sleeves over her hands to hide the red-rust crescent moons of each unclean fingertip.

to strike or meet a surface
(as after a fall)

Hand-in-hand we cross the Sears parking lot. My grandfather looks down at seven-year-old me and says, *You're my favorite.* Maybe he says that to all his eleven grandkids, but after a happy pause between us, he clears his throat and follows those words with what seems a sincere request. *Let's keep that our secret.* And I do. I did. I kept it tucked in my pocket like an apple seed, its soft topaz aglow.

At my excommunication, the men sat with me around several, long fold-up tables used for Family Potluck Sunday. I was nineteen and the only woman in the room. Only girl. My oldest brother and my father sat to my left. My bereft grandfather caressed the pages of an open Bible across from me.

Every man spoke his piece. Each stated his concern for my soul, substantiated with a Bible verse or personal experiences of God's punishment or the Devil's cunning. When my grandfather spoke, he shook his head and said through tears, *You were the apple of my eye.*

I'd been with the boy for nearly a year. We strolled the orchard near the farm where he volunteered. No one knew me anymore and I belonged nowhere. Except with this boy. Our love was enough. Under those fruit-laden trees he told me he'd been thinking, and he was coming to believe that monogamy wasn't natural. What did I think about his having several wives? *But you,* he said, *would always be my favorite.*

I meet the clay mud ground with the sound of a kiss. Soiled reflection in the pupil of my grandfather's eye. I'm past tense. In present and in future I'm fallen like Eve, like the apples she didn't pick that let go to earth at season's change.

I strike loam where once flowed a boundless spring.

a portion of the earth's solid surface distinguishable by boundaries or ownership

Canada: just foreign enough to not be the United States: there, southwest side of the strait: my mountains: Olympus, Townsend, The Brothers, Mount Deception: mirages: a stone's throw away from these Dallas Road cliffs I walk: my legs belong to me, my body: half my father/half my mother: the girl in me (a)part: not far enough or close enough home: I crossed lines to get here: Canada: my second birthplace: where, for the first time, my eyes open to unbelonging: those are not *my* mountains: range of peaks and future glimpses: I see churches surrender daughters: when asked *who gives this woman's hand?* they answer: and the whole of her body: I didn't know my body, what is mine: to give away: to take from: remember back to: afterthought agreements in the far west: who took this portion of the earth's solid surface differs from who took that part: who ceded without defining *own*: Nuu-chah-nulth, Makah, Coast Salish: walking this land, now: I see whales where there are no whales: ocean's deep ungiven: unknown, unclaimed bodies: negotiating wing kelp and liquid borders–

to bring to a landing
(a perfect–, crash–)

My life became storm. I didn't return to university the fall after my first year. The I-90 floating bridge sank due to heavy rains and human error. My brother married my best friend. The Persian Gulf War began. I accompanied the boy to Co-Dependence Anonymous and kept going back. Though we seriously planned our future together, the boy proposed in a half-joking questionnaire which I never filled out and returned.

...will you marry me, and have me as your most excellent and hilarious, lawful wedded husband forever and ever, Ahmen? ☐ Yes ☐ No ☐ Oh, go on ☐ Other. Please specify:

He moved to Seattle and lived with me and a high school friend in a small apartment in the U District until he had a nervous breakdown culminating in suicidal depression and returned to Metchosin, placing us in a holding pattern.

In severe weather, pilots make go-rounds. That is, they decide it safer to climb back into sky rather than continue to land. During our relationship, the boy had expressed many times that he wished I had more sexual experience. While we were separated–circling the possibility of life apart–I gathered experience. Our final breakup began in earnest when I told him I slept with someone in a field of tall dry grass. I wanted to hurt the boy, but I also wanted to please him. I wanted to land in the life he first wanted for us on an organic farm with a gang of *fucking cute kids*. I could not tell if I loved the boy or if I needed him. If I didn't have him, then who did I have, and why did I cause so much turbulence in my life?

I crashed in brambles sharp with guilt and regret and fear of death. It would take years to pick free the thorns. I failed to save the boy and lost myself in the attempt. I lost all the men in my life by loving the wrong one.

After I climbed back into the sky as the boy's *friend*, I nose-dived into the sea where the specter of Hell, of my eternal separation from God and my family, clung to my dreams as the last vestige of my indoctrination. Though fear of Hell was not enough to return me to church, I lived like a whale with aching hipbones. I swam away from the crash site as remnants of walking life on a tortured shore dissolved with each rebirth.

COUNTRY
(mother–, father–)

I come from a mother who never wanted to leave Minnesota. After high school graduation, she fled her parents' new home in Seattle and returned to Duluth–her birthplace–where she fell in love with my father.

I come from a father who convinced my mother to venture with him back West. Though he loves his hometown, he has always said Duluth was a good place to be *from*.

In my motherland you can travel years on a longing for Lake Superior *so big you can't see the other side*. Like an ocean–but it's not. Meanwhile, the Salish Sea swells but thirty minutes from your front door.

In my fatherland you believe you belong because you haul, stack, and chop wood, work a belt sander, drive stick-shift. You follow cousins and uncles with everything strapped to your back for miles, switchbacking high valleys through trees and tight-rope walking mountainside goat trail vistas. Nights outside your tent, you breathe ghosts under the dot-to-dot night firmament.

My mother is a place I hated to leave, until I did. And then I left often and haphazardly. A place I returned to many times until soon after my meeting with the churchmen when she said, *I miss you*–though I sat across her table. *You're here*, she mourned. *But you're not really here.* We had become countries unrecognizable to each other.

My father is a place I didn't think I'd ever leave because he was always there, until he wasn't. He sat next to me at the table with the churchmen, but he was not *with* me.

They call my parents' country of origin the Land of Ten Thousand Lakes. There you'll find a lake shaped for every dream you've ever rowed across. *L'Étoile du Nord*, they say. A star not north but center of our continent. The place from which legendary pioneers set forth or settled. My parents on the couch surrounded by pajamaed children, watching Little House on the Prairie every Monday night at 8:00pm Pacific Standard Time. *Take me back*, my mother wishes. Instead, we dwell long years in Michael Landon's Walnut Grove, memorizing Hollywood histories as if they are true.

ground or soil of a specified situation, nature, or quality

Warning: Mudflow ahead.

I'm a seismographer measuring the nature of my underground disturbances in hindsight.

I created mudflows without meaning to, and rode them to new, unplanned formations of rock and earth.

I didn't follow signs marking the evacuation route and became a river uplifted, churned and set on a new course, forged new ruts while old self debris heaved down the mountainside.

Watershed revised.

Maybe I always felt it coming.

Before May 18, 1980, Mount Saint Helens (Lawetlat'la to the Cowlitz people, and Loowit to the Klickitat) erupted as recently as 150 years ago. In fact, as an active stratovolcano–ever building new layers of hardened lava, pumice, ash, and miscellaneous fragments–Saint Helens' history of eruptive activity stretches back over 40,000 years.

It doesn't matter whether or not we know the nature or tendencies of the land we live on. We distress when ground we thought solid shifts, erupts, and buries us in ash.

Down-feather soft.

Fine as smoke.

We collected Saint Helens ash by the coffee canfull

from the ground and trees around my grandparents' cabin, which resembled those old black and white photographs hand-tinted in muted color.

That summer a lifeguard stood at the edge of the community pool pleading,

Get out! Go home! St. Helens blew again!

We fled in just our swimsuits and towels around our waists.

Warm ash descended from blue sky to speckle our chlorine-scented backs as we kicked up gray clouds on the forest trail leading back to the A-frame safety of our grandparents' home.

Though I feared the power of the earth, the Devil, and the rapture that would come as a thief in the night, I felt safe. My connection to a named God layered weekly at church into my private lithosphere of faith in Jesus, in being truly forgiven and loved at a mysteriously subterranean level. On the surface, though, I sensed a perimeter.

An octagon.

The night-rained, moss-caked gazebo in Mt. Olivet pioneer cemetery near my parents' house where for the first time I kissed a boy, my hands inside his tattered leather jacket against his thermo shirt. He loved me certainly. Wrote me long, poetic, tightly-folded notes from his heart that he pressed into my hand between classes in our high school hallways. My fear of our love culminated in the warmth of his encircling arms, our kiss in that decaying cemetery gazebo.

Even then I was afraid to love outside my church, so as a preventative measure, I broke up with him. After all, how could I–a child who had secretly always loved my human father more than I loved my hidden-faced Heavenly Father–be strong enough to love God more than Man?

Love not the world, neither the things that are in the world. If any man (or woman?) *love the world, the love of the Father is not in him* (or her?). *For all that is in the world, the lust of the flesh, and the lust of the eyes, and the pride of life, is not of the Father, but is of the world. And the world passeth away, and the lust thereof: but he* (or she?) *that doeth the will of God abideth forever.*

In my core, I knew my world would pass away if I loved a man outside my church. Or was it lust? In my core, I knew my world would pass away if I lusted after–gave my body to–a man outside my church, outside the circle of words that Pastor spoke me into.

How red our faces –Hilary, me, and Pastor's daughter–in the catechism class where Pastor made us write down the less obvious sins against the Sixth Commandment:

filthy talk or gestures
immodest clothing
dance:
    a. suggestive movements of the body
    b. the close embrace of unmarried couples

necking
petting
lustful looks or glances
homosexuality

It wasn't my nature to dig at the roots of my Sunday School groundwork or to record the rumblings I sensed in Luther's Small Catechism. Or, if it was my nature, I developed a second-guess reflex to cast doubt on my doubts, to fossilize them in a bedrock of shame.

In that same stone– the memory of being the only girl to join in flag football in a Skyway playfield after Sunday Service. Girl who could outrun the church's young men and boys. Girl who scored touchdowns–a red flag flying from each hip.

You should be at home in the kitchen where you belong, fumed the organist, Pastor's most disgruntled son. *Brother,* my brother said. *That's not cool.* Pastor's son wrote an apology note and on the following Sunday handed it not to me, but to my brother–a man who spoke for me but did not say what I wanted to say. But what would I have said?

How would I have said it?
If
your voice
is
a closed
um-
brella

how
do you speak?

Oh, I wish I could've heard my
Great Grandma Ellis' waterproof voice! My father once
told me that back in the Missouri Synod disintegration
days his grandmother brought a sturdy, hook-handled
umbrella and sat in the back of the room at the monthly
Voter's Meeting, where women were not allowed to
speak or vote on church issues. When she disagreed
with what the men said, my great grandmother jack-
hammered the metal tip of her umbrella against the
floor. In this way the church men heard her thunder.

That thunder raps in my blood, too. Yet my voice began
as drizzle–a static, morning sound when fog and
electricity collide. Hymnal hums and the flickering buzz
of bible verses connecting in the right sockets to light
some dimness in my sinful human heart. My biggest
dare:

God-dear,
please hear
my unscripted
prayer.

When my nineteen-year-old voice was a closed
umbrella, I picked it up and opened it with questions I
had never thought before.

How do we know there is a god?

Science will not tell you that open umbrellas trigger volcanoes and mudslides. But I know they do.

What I was really asking was how do we know the blond-haired, blue-eyed Jesus and the white-haired, white-robed, old Father, and the Holy unsexed, background Ghost combine to be the true Triune God for all people? When they said the Bible tells us so, I wondered why I should believe words written, compiled, and interpreted by men who are enabled and empowered by their own interpretations of those words. And when they said a person can choose to *not* believe but they cannot choose to believe, I felt the magma glow of my unspeakable beliefs begin to rise. The seismograph's ink on a scroll of paper drawing a new distinction between indoctrination and faith.

My Christian faith was as blind as a man with apples for eyes, while my personal connection to God– my understanding of a presence bigger and more complicated than man–dwelt in me unseen but in clean focus.

I felt this truth, but I did not give it authority because I was cast as Girl/ Lamb, born into Pastor/Shepard's power to describe my faith for me.

My hidden need to define my own truth
confirmed my innate hubris.
My new desire to question

pointed to an inevitable shame by virtue of my sex.

My questions signaled alarm.

Martin Luther, Martin Luther!
Half the world still hears you
pounding nails to affix your
95 Theses to the Wittenberg Castle Church door. Each blow a protest, protest with each blow. You thundered against Catholic priests who assured the masses that good works and the purchase of indulgences can lead to salvation, even for the dead.

Hammer clamber.
A necessary moment in the examination and reformation of man-made rules. A reminder of divine grace for those with empty pockets and an overfull conscience.

There grew the divide.

Does it matter
if the hammer
is a myth?

Historians agree that
Martin Luther never
nailed the 95 Theses
to the Castle Church door
or to any door.

Does it matter
if the umbrella
is a myth?

When recently asked,
my father did not verify
the story of my
great grandmother's
waterproof voice.

Does it matter if the tide
against abuse of indulgences
and papal rule rose
all around Luther? He wrote
a list of ninety-five points
to discuss with fellow
priests and bishops. He
didn't intend his questions
to trigger a mudslide
powerful enough
to shear away purgatory,
indulgences and intercessors
(saint of this and that,
Virgin Mary and the ears
of priests in the confessionals)
making straight our path
to God. Luther's mudflow
stripped the pope
of his authority over souls.
For this he was
excommunicated.

Does it matter if the tide of my
doubts rose the year
prior to my leaving the
country? One Saturday
while in Bellingham
visiting a friend's
boyfriend, he
professed himself an atheist.
The night ended in a tearful
phone call to my friend's father
asking how to convince
unbelievers that God exists.
I returned next morning in time
for church and whispered in
the bathroom to Hilary before
Bible History class if she
thought it possible that man
invented God and religion.
Voicing questions, seeking
answers—was it for this I was
excommunicated?

A division that continues to divide.

One foot in the Middle Ages and one unwitting foot in
the Renaissance, Martin Luther—as we often say about
heroes who lacked respect for and awareness of universal
human worth—was a product of his time. He surmised
God created women with broad hips so they could sit in

the home. He sided with princes and nobles against peasants and farmers who wanted a societal Revolution to accompany the emerging spiritual Reformation for freedom and equity. To him, the Islamic people were the Devil's punishment for Christians who didn't continue attending church after they were told attending church didn't guarantee Heaven. He fueled hatred of Jews and anabaptists, by advocating that their worldly goods be seized; that they be dragged from their places of worship

    and burned.

          Another

      man

  un-

   ravels.

        Another di-

           vision that continues

to divide

    five hundred years later in a small side street church:

    July heat trapped in the daylight basement where a young women outwardly denounces Jesus as her Savior

      and becomes separate.

Separation for eternity.

         The last claim my church had on me was fear of eternal separation from God and from my family when upon death I would descend to Hell, while they would ascend to dwell before the face of God in Heaven. I would also suffer eternal torture mostly involving fire. Pastor's kindest son encouraged me to read Dante's *Inferno* so I could get a concrete picture of what was in store for me.

I never did.

Under my tongue, I kept a question like an ember: *Do my parents truly believe I will not be with them in Heaven?* I still don't ask because I know they carry that belief and grief like a pocketful of nuclear waste.

Cruel, ugly, and unprovable though it is, my guaranteed Hell-bound afterlife made sense to me back then. After all, I willfully turned my back on the salvation and truth given me in childhood whereas some people never find and hold that salvation.

But fear of Hell had always lived in me like the petroleum pipeline buried in our backyard.

My fear flowed,
--------------------------invisible-------------------------
undercurrents ascended.
When I left the church
the church left me
with gnashing teeth and sulfur-stained sheets
that I sorted and washed
with the rest of my fraying laundry.

In the year following my excommunication,

108

I had the wherewithal to see a therapist though I could barely afford it. She said everything I told her about leaving the church seemed right on time for me. Maybe you're a late bloomer, she said, but some degree of separation or rebellion from our parents' beliefs is part of becoming a unique individual. I was offended. How could my questions and heresy be a normal part of most every human's life when the ground beneath my feet had turned to slurry and pieces of myself disintegrated and dispersed? I stopped seeing her. I told myself I had to choose between therapy or groceries, but I know it's because I didn't feel special enough in her eyes. Gradually, I found comfort in my therapist's assessment. My separation milestones happened in my own time, in my own way. I'm not more or less special than anyone else.

I was raised to feel special, accepted, and loved in my concentric circles: family, church, neighborhood, and privileged, middle-class society. My whole country consistently uplifts white, Christian specialness. And in my ignorance, I believed I was special.

Until I wasn't.

The ground of my belonging shifted on conditions of obedience to male spiritual authority. Submission a quicksand made more deadly by resistance. Silence a clay to shape the vessel which entombs a raging tongue. The moment I slipped into this world, the church plowed the unconditional holding ground of Original Love and sowed the seeds of Original Sin.

Maybe I was bound to fall away
so that I could tell you, my daughter:

we spin in the same breeze
as dangling catkins and fall leaves.

We are mudflow and driveway puddle.
We are a forest reduced to pick-up-sticks,
stripped, and flattened in the blast zone.

We are avalanche lily.
We are the newborn shape of Spirit Lake.

We are ant and pocket gopher,
moss, and dwarf bramble.

We are prairie lupine and fireweed
setting root until red alder and sitka willow make canopy for sword and lady fern, for wild wood sorrel.

We all live like mountains:

our family, friends,
spiritual practices, school, work, and country are layers of a strato-history that may gather underground for our lifetime or wake us with a shattering disruption.

And like every being on the planet,

daughter, you are singular.

A season like no other.

COUNTRY
(home–)

When you were born, I was seen again.

My parents watched me expand my way to motherhood arriving with you, their eighth grandchild. I imagine they saw the chance you might bring me back to church. I know they hoped I would bring you to the baptismal font. And I saw my parents again through you–the fear and desire that your child be safe in mind, body, soul. As I write this, your grandparents–my mother and father– are still living. They are old and suffer health issues, so my brothers, sisters, and I care for them as if they are our children.

Your father and I used to take you to the San Juan Islands at Christmas when you were little and couldn't protest. Our families hated your absence. We'd splurge on a room at Rosario's on Orcas, where we draped colorful strings of lights and decorated a tiny fake tree with ribbons and mini metallic balls, our room warm and flickering in fire light.

My own Holy Family holding ground and being held.

There's a soaking pool at Rosario's, in the basement of the grand mansion where it's dark and salty.

                                        I'm often there again,

afloat.

A single, sea star

slow spin

tuning in
     to the dim-lit water.

Buoyed by salt.

Fatherless.   Motherless.

It is the biggest circle.

There I have no inflatable boat or borrowed oars, but it is the same water–the same substance of my faith–that I rowed across in my parents' old backyard where the vine maple samaras propel to earth and land as a child or a tree.

to set down after conveying

You live on an island now. We moved to this new home against your will. I feared your anger and resistance to this change. I worried your father and I made a selfish decision that would ruin your life and our connection to you. But you have decorated your new room, learned the roads and forest paths, moved through circles at school and still visit friends on the mainland. You always come home to us, though I brace for the time you don't, and I stretch my faith to believe our separation over time will be gradual as the carving of great canyons.

Do you remember I promised you bunnies when we moved here? Bought a hutch (we never used) for the side of the house near your bedroom. Now we toy with the idea of goats.

Maybe I wanted you to feel what I felt, tending creatures in my care that still-dark, frosty November morning before school. I carried rabbit food and a pitcher of hot water to melt the ice I knew had formed in the rabbits' water bowl.

The full moon hung in the diamond fog just high enough to not tangle in the swooping cables and crisscross steelwork of our ever-buzzing power tower.

The moon's presence illuminated the glorious selection of trees dotting our Garden of Eden.

It was the first of many times I sensed the strength of moon as Holy Ghost, electrifying my deepest self, gathering the reserves I would need for my future as a young woman growing up on this planet on the cusp of the next millennium.

The thing is, I don't know what will speak to you and show you the way. There are as many paths to God as there are people. All I have is my faith in love and its power to provide us with strength to survive and thrive past times of separation and division. I can't guarantee your happiness, or safety, or the outcomes of your decisions. But I can urge you to ask questions, ask questions, ask questions and to welcome uncertain answers. To *hug and release*, like your kindergarten teacher said to do when we left you at school. Like the recorded voice on the commuter boat says every time we leave home and cross the water: *Please hold onto seatbacks and handrails when moving about the vessel. Always be ready for unexpected movement.*

This is what I want to tell you.

Chapter Home

you and I became us

September 12th

And if the bowl were stronger, my story had been longer.
–Mother Goose's "Three Wise Men of Gotham City"

It was not easy clawing up the coast to home.

Deming, New Mexico: we waited
outside the unmanned station
for a train that never came.

We spent the day under a spell
of loudspeakers and shopkeepers
who barely noticed our presence,
our tourist's shine worn off
in the dirt and rock of our torn country.

We sleep-marched through the town museum
corridors teeming with dead histories, eyes
of antique dolls little mirrors of you and me.

We memorized tacked-up signs that told us
almost a thousand years ago the Mimbres
buried their dead with a punctured bowl
pressed over the face–spirits slipped through
jagged openings to the afterlife.

Dragged home in a thread of silver passenger cars
we felt the kneel of skyscrapers under the weight
of death, while hours passed into a darkness

which became the time called *post–*

Wake: Post–

We lie all night with our eyes to the cold November sky, watching meteors pop and ping like glass bits from a distant, shattered window. Winter dampness fills every corner of our lakeside cabin. We huddle together under a stratification of blankets, our heads at the foot of the bed for a better view of outer space. I sleep and waken, startled by a lunging flash in the star-infested sky. Meteors with blazing white tails of light sailing dangerously close to the surface of our world become a dream we corroborate hours before dawn.

Contort: Pre–

You once travelled across the country with a mishmash of people to the Big Apple. Dead Heads. A mother with a small tribe of children. Runaway teenagers. A Turkish man told you about prayer rugs and disappeared five times a day–sometimes mid-conversation–to keep his regular devotions. You smoked pot with a guy from Olympia, a *Greener* who thought maybe he remembered you from one of his classes though you'd been to Evergreen State College ten years before him. Two nights and three days, coach-class train Seattle to New York, your spine never so contorted.

Even in that time before *us*, you belonged everywhere. Your shape fit people you met like a shadow. Opposite of explosion, you radiated calm. Settled dust.

Enter: Post–

Deming, New Mexico. The *Southwest Chief* never arrives and an automated voice on Amtrak's phone system tells us there's a nine-hour delay, a twelve-hour delay. We pay to enter the old customhouse restored as the Deming Luna Mimbres Museum. In each nine-hundred-year-old Mimbres bowl a small bulletburst hole cracks through the clay. I ask whether you remember the rhyme about the three wise men of Gotham City who went to sea in a bowl:

If the bowl were stronger, my story would be longer.

Join: Pre–

Our journey from Washington State to New Mexico did
not in any way resemble your trip to New York, except
we also moved by train. We were each other's shadow–
joined at the hip as my mother said of close friends.
Other than the man from Portland bent on selling us
a probiotic supplement drink, we talked only to each
other. For this trip, you splurged on a private room
with a long bench that unfolded to a bed, a table that
hinged flat under the window, and a phone-booth-size
bathroom where we showered together like nascent,
fearless twins wrapped around each other in a swaying
womb.

Escape: Post–

You stand before the zigzag-patterned bowls tapping the side of your head as if inviting your skull's door to open. I bend to read the age-curled sign taped inside the display case:

Nearly one thousand years ago, the peoples of the Mimbres Valley of New Mexico produced many ceramic vessels with painted images of birds, humans, and other animals.

Many bowls have been discovered in the ruins of adobe homes, in subfloor pits dug to hold a body in fetal position where they were placed over the face of the deceased.

The bowls you see here are pierced, or "killed." The significance of such kill-holes is unclear. Explanations for them range from rendering the bowls useless to allowing their spirit, or that of the deceased, to escape.

I tap my breastbone as if testing the box that shields my heart and lungs. How long do the dead listen to their family cook and clean and dream as air flows out and back through the nostrils of the living?

Suspend: Pre–

On Vancouver Island, the Tla-o-qui-aht used to raise their dead to the first branches of a sitka spruce as if the soul was something the trees could take. A once-loved body placed on wooden planks. Lifted out of human reach and sight. I had no business being there on an island a short row from the village of Tofino where rests the rotted outline of a longhouse beaten and carried off by storms. I wanted a photograph for a museum in my mind. I should have been old enough to know the soul is something a camera can take. In the forest, under the suspended wooden platform, a stream barely simmered. Moss enfolded a human skull, tilted in the silt. Cobalt beads and dentalium shells. Everything pulled to earth, unstrung, and scattered.

Circle: Post–

We rode the rails through light and dark. You have heard my stories from the time before. You know my landmarks, water names, and places I made home. Now this cabin next to this lake. You row, and I see the oars as clumsy, skeletal extensions of your arms drawing circles half immersed, half arcing the surface. We have not lived every season here to know when the stars are bright enough or the lake still enough to mimic a night sky. But we will.

Witness: Pre–

If all light is the white seeds of night, flecks of planet glass and pins of bright flying rock, if a desert dissolves into darkness, if a city has yet to exist, or flashbulbs, light-emitting diodes, match strikes or lanterns for hurricanes–then overhead, then sky, then looking up is all there is to do.

For twenty-three days, beginning July 5, 1054–well before colonization or our country's English written history–the Mimbres people witnessed a supernova dangle from the tip of a crescent moon. Halfway round the world, in China and Japan, astronomers noted this event in songs and sacred etchings.

The Mimbres, too, documented what they saw. Someone fashioned a clay bowl and painted its sides with a black-and-white, twenty-three-pointed star near a rabbit shaped as a crescent moon, surrounded by an altered sky.

Hold: Post–

The headlines are not carved in stone though they say *None of Us Will Ever Forget*. They say *Disbelief, Terrible Sadness and a Quiet Unyielding Anger*. In another decade we build a monument within the footprint of the lost towers. A bowl that will not hold.

Define: Pre–

You'd planned a train trip for us and I came from the bedroom where I'd been packing, where two words clunked around my mind like rocks hitting a garden shovel: *trepination* and *trepidation*.

You stood at your drafting table, an indigo oil pastel pinched between your fingers as you stared at the face staring up at you from the paper. For months you'd been contemplating the lines of faces, how they extend past the boundaries of bone in arcs and distant intersections.

I knew one word was fear of what comes next, but the other–

Trepination? The carpet under your sneakers streaked with ground-in chips of red and blue and turquoise; a stout, ceramic mug muddied with coffee ready at the small table beside you. I knew you didn't want to explain, *When they thought people were insane or possessed? Well, medieval doctors drilled a small hole in a person's head to let the devil out.*

You traded an oil pastel for your cup of coffee, took a sip, asked, *Are you afraid something bad will happen?*

Desert: Post–

The ticket seller at the bus depot in Las Cruces tells me there is something bad happening in New York. I slip quarters into the vending machine, choose a Twix for the road, and think how people everywhere overreact to news. Now she says there is something bad happening in Washington, D.C. I thank her, take our tickets, walk outside, and wait next to you. On the Greyhound from Las Cruces to Deming we stare out at dry landscape occasionally dotted with facades of old western town facades that may have once been thriving strip malls but now resemble real ghost towns. I tell you something bad might be happening. We watch the desert roll by, complete with tumbleweeds.

Close: Pre–

For three days and two early September nights in Red River, New Mexico we slept with the motel's sliding glass door open. Moving water exhaled midnight, into predawn, twilight, sunrise, day. One afternoon we wandered the town and imagined what it would be like to buy the little motel for sale across from Bull o' the Woods Saloon. We pretended to explain evergreens and tide pools to our landlocked, someday-child, born here unacquainted with ocean waves or living, looming columns of hemlock and spruce. It was the first time we spoke our future together. When we noticed signs posted on every telephone pole warning of a wild bear that MAY COME CHARGING, we knew without saying we could not feel safe in a town that shared its streets with such wild animals. That night we slid the door closed against that river's red breath.

Peer: Post–

Jagged *ker pow!* shapes in the windows of the unmanned train depot. Plywood nailed over doorways. We've waited the day in the museum, the library, the corner café. Somewhere down the line train cars stand like a row of cattle while dogs sniff for bombs and agents sniff for shifty looks, turbans, or abandoned packages. No one knows what they're looking for. We peer down the tracks through the New Mexico night and finally spot the engine's headlights like a gamboling satellite headed our direction. Soon the roaring vessel stops at our feet with violent reluctance. A conductor ushers us up into the car.

But this is not our train.

Not our train because

nobody boarding and nobody riding is sure

who is who

is we is us

is them.

Float: Pre–

High above ground, I worked summers–or whenever I needed travel money–as a temp on the forty-second floor of the Wells Fargo Building downtown Seattle. Data entry. Double tall lattes. At the north windows, where I alphabetized forms and filed by last name, I tracked Interstate 5's thread as far as I could see, remembered its stretch to Canada. Headphones, photocopies. "Cigarettes and Chocolate Milk" in my ear. Cup-o-Soup in the florescent-lit break room overlooking the wired city grid. In the south distance, hidden roads to the A-frame cabin where my forest grandparents no longer lived. Spreadsheet formulas. Labels jammed in printers. Envelopes, stuffed, sealed, dropped in the mail room. Even on the blusteriest days, I know there stands the mountain I've always thought of as Great Mother for the way her arms stretch wide enough to hold the sassy city and its crammed lakeshores, burgeoning suburbs, and still bridges afloat.

Splinter: Post–

Though it's well past midnight, passengers talk excitedly about the *attack on our own soil–our own soil!* They eye us warily as we settle into our seats. *Someone's gotta pay. Who could have done such a thing to* us?

You sleep. The train window reflects your neck, odd angle bent. When I close my eyes I feel myself skyscraper high typing strings of numbers on a keypad, my ears full of croon and electric guitar to pass the hours until the windows splinter–

    and a fleeting nebula of paperclips

and the black hole under my desk

    industrial carpet soft as cement

and my hands are not my own
    but a woman who paints her nails Plugged-In Plum

she observes the trajectory of office shrapnel
    paper flowers afire

tower windows that should not open–
    Ker pow!
        through which a soul could escape.

Reverberate: Pre–

Last time I left Canada, I crossed the border at Peace Arch with my father and all my belongings in his old truck. I didn't stay home long. By winter, my Canadian friend and I were lurching by train out of Amsterdam and crossing Europe into Istanbul.

For months we woke to *Fajr*, dawn prayer reverberating from thousands of mosques throughout the city. We walked the Bosphorus from Europe to Asia, touched land in Ephesus. I'd never felt so out of my place. North America was sloughing off me like rat-chewed fiberglass insulation. And underneath bloomed common and plentiful accepted invitations into homes and carpet shops where my friend and I sat for hours with strangers' eyes meeting us from the rims of clear glass teacups.

My family feared I was gone for good. My friend's mother worried we would become some man's chattel. I began dreaming in Turkish, forgot the order of my mother tongue. I pretended not to understand my friend finally telling me I had nowhere else to go but home.

Empty: Post–

The sky changed. Not just for three days after–when
earthbound people glutted airport terminals, crowded
in buses, or in rooms thought safe and unreachable–
but for weeks and months the sky remained empty
of rabbits and loons, star nits and whale plume. We
could make nothing of the clouds. We rarely looked up
because we didn't know, couldn't guess, what the sky
would hold, what the moon would next resemble.

Ignite: Pre–

On the *Coast Starlight* from Seattle to Los Angeles, water, sand, swamp and land veined westward out our train window. Everything remembered thrummed:

We met head-on crossing Cherry Street at the lunch hour. You carried a Styrofoam box crammed with Indian food, wore your canvas coat with a Las Vegas McCarron International Airport patch over the heart–later I would learn your aunt's boyfriend worked there and had left his coat when he left your aunt. We said hello because we knew each other through mutual friends, for the past eight years connected at various shows or parties. You walked backward with me to the side of the street you'd just come from and asked me to jot my phone number on the top of your take-out box. You watched the ink dig into the warm Styrofoam like I engraved something sacred.

Telephone lines an electrocardiogram of our unhurried arrival in Los Angeles. Did my pulse rate seek to mimic yours? Did our matching pulses match the beat of rail wheels on track? You said we became *us* right then on Cherry Street. A gentle ignition, followed by *purrrrrrr*.

Search: Post–

We learned new stories behind old words: Boxcutter. Anthrax. Suspicious packages. Shoe bomb. Guantanamo. Slam dunk. We watched televised speeches and funerals as firemen kicked up toxic soot on Liberty Street. Posters of the missing swelled like lichen on temporary chainlink fences. We marched against the war even as we bought tickets to Paris the year after the towers fell. Bagdad burned on the tiny TV in our sparse hotel room. We rented a cheap *apartmento* in Ericera, Portugal, where we waited out the wind and read of a new virus spreading in China. In debt and desperation, we searched without luck for any kind of work in Ireland, until we knew we couldn't stay gone.

Mottle: Pre–

In the moon's elevations and craters, the Mimbres of New Mexico saw a leaping rabbit. And in Japan, legend tells of an old man lost and starving in the forest, who meets a rabbit. The rabbit offers herself as a meal by hopping into the cooking fire. As it happens, the old man is a god so moved by the rabbit's selfless act, he places her in the moon to be that light for all eternity.

Moon became rabbit.

Rabbit became moon.

Elsewhere on our globe, a tree, a smiling woman, or a toad appeared in relief upon the bright moon's mottled surface. In ancient India, a pair of hands. Which came first: our stories or the moon?

Face: Post–

I can't remember September 11 without remembering the meteor shower we witnessed two months later when we lay in our bed near the lake. I can't see a rabbit in the face of the full moon, only a man–exhaling smoke or howling in time to the electric buzz of the powerlines in my childhood backyard.

I can't think of Cherry Street, or Indian food in Styrofoam containers, without believing–

you and I became *us.*

Ring: Pre–

When I was a sapling, my family looped Mount Rainier
to reach my grandparents' cabin in the woods. In summer,

we arced northeast to south through Enumclaw and Green-
water when Chinook and Cayuse opened clear and passable.

Our winter slog returned us southwest to north through
bustling logging towns: Eatonville, Morton, Randle.

In the Grove of the Patriarchs, my father showed us kids
how nurse logs gave birth to a new generation of giants.

I had already left home, already been excommunicated
from my family's church when my father cut down

the ailing alder trees in our backyard. I kept a small round
like a relic in the steam trunk I hauled from place to place

through my university years. Let me show you how to start
from heartwood and count rings outward past sapwood,

cambium, outer bark, to the unseen
                              chain of circles that connect us.

Prepare: Post–

From which *now* does everything become *after?*

Birth

We have a due date.

We cast a moon in clay from the shape of my globe belly.

We have a birth date.

We paint this bowl the color of our daughter's eyes.

We are joined at the hip by a new light, a new shape.

Gaze: Post–

You will sketch the shapes of impossible structures, the lines of which extend to outer space like fishing rods over a lake. I will stand away from the warm cabin to test the theory that the longer a person gazes into the night sky the more stars come to light on the person's eyes. We will tell our daughter how we vowed each other married with a clink of half-full pints in a Galway pub. She will point out deer or dog in the bowl of the moon.

Spiral: Pre–

We read of explosions in other countries. We anticipate the eruption of our mountains, our neighborhoods and coworkers. We attend Winter Concert at the elementary school where a timid choir sings of burning leaves that carpet forest floors. We watch wormholes spiral in sci-fi movies like a hypnotist's voice among clots and shards of eternal interplanetary debris. We brace for new variants of an old disease. And through the shortest nights, we store tangled strings of lights in our shadow rafters.

Notes

Chapter Water

4 **Running in the Family by flashlight in the parking lot**: I loved every Michael Ondaatje book. *Running in the Family* (1982, W. W. Norton) is a fictionalized memoir about Ondaatje's late 1970s return to Sri Lanka, his country of origin.

6 **the L.A. Race Riots explode**: Hearing about and seeing Rodney King's beating while in Canada reinforced a naïve perception that I was personally removed from racism even as my country steeped in it. While this book is not about racism in the United States, it is about the ability of every individual to examine what we have been taught and what we have believed about ourselves and others since childhood. Statistics in this piece come from:
http://www.southcentralhistory.com/la-riots.php

11 **peaceful protest, or simply Clayoquot Summer**: Friends of Clayoquot Sound provides a timeline of these events here: http://www.focs.ca/about-us/history/

13 **Starhawk will hold a spiral dance at sunset:** When Starhawk arrived in Clayoquot Sound in 1993, I knew nothing about her. Though I still don't know much, I have since read the introduction to the 20th Anniversary Edition of *Spiral Dance* (1999, HarperOne) and connected with Starhawk's statement that she has always wanted "to challenge the spiritual supremacy of patriarchal males and male images."

15 **my father's church said not to partake in the Sin of Unionism**: In confirmation class, we hand-wrote and

memorized the following definitions on one of the blank pages of our catechism: The Sin of Unionism is "the joining together in religious work and worship with those who are not one in faith." The Sin of Syncretism is "the joining together in religious works and worship on the part of professing Christians and professing heathens."

18 **these remote protests:** On the 25th anniversary of the protests (2018), the Sierra Club wrote: "The protests in Clayoquot Sound, led by Indigenous leaders and supported by thousands of concerned citizens, made international headlines as the largest act of civil disobedience in the history of Canada. As a result of the protests, the BC government had to change course and give up its plan to allow logging of the majority of the region's old-growth rainforest. In 2017, the Ahousaht First Nation announced a land use vision seeking Indigenous protected areas for the majority of their territory." Though these events felt victorious at the time because they raised world-wide awareness and helped preserve the rainforest of Clayoquot Sound, the other ninety per cent of Vancouver Island was intensely logged. https:// sierraclub. bc.ca/25-years-after-the-clayoquot-sound-protests-vancouver-islands-remaining-old-growth-rainforest-is-still-disappearing/

But activists have not given up. The protests on September 9, 2021, at Fairy Creek, on southwestern Vancouver Island, surpassed the protests at Clayoquot Sound as the largest act of civil disobedience in Canadian history, with 882 arrests. There is still work to do to protect these trees and our future. http://www.wltribune.com/news/fairy-creek-arrests-surpass-1000-in-canadas-largest-act-of-civil-disobedience/

20 **a bloodless battle:** The National Parks Service provides

a brief history of The Pig War and the making of the water border in the San Juan Islands here: http://www.nps.gov/sajh/learn/historyculture/the-pig-war.htm

27 **a book grown more powerful and useful to me than the weighty King James Bible:** *Daughters of Copper Woman*, Anne Cameron (1981, Harbour Publishing)

27 **the silent role of women**: In Catechism class, we memorized "let your women keep silence in the churches: for it is not permitted unto them to speak; but they are commanded to be under obedience, as also saith the law. And if they will learn anything, let them ask their husbands at home: for it is a shame for women to speak in the church" (I Corinthians 14:34-35 KJV), which laid to rest any doubt about how a woman may or may not use her voice in the church. And if we wanted to understand why women are forbidden the role of pastor and are not allowed to vote on church issues, we could recall the memorized verse "let the woman learn in silence with all subjection. But suffer not a woman to teach, nor to usurp authority over the man, but to be in silence" (1 Timothy 2:11-12 KJV). However, women in our church were permitted to teach Sunday School, and my grandmother taught Bible History.

33 **everything remotely useful:** Morton, Arthur S. and Lewis G Thomas. *A History of the Canadian West to 1870-71* (2nd ed.). Toronto, Ontario: University of Toronto Press, 1973, p. 404.

Chapter Land

41 **a course maintained for seventy-five years:** The first Princess Marguerite sailed *The Triangle Route* between Seattle, Vancouver, and Victoria from 1925-1941. Two other Marguerites sailed the route from Seattle to Victoria for another forty-eight years. I had the pleasure of travelling between Seattle and Victoria many times aboard the Vancouver Island Princess, which took over this route during my university years.

"Seattle Steam Ferry Lands in Retirement", The Bulletin, Bend, Oregon. September 18, 1989
https://www.historylink.org/File/7478
https://mynorthwest.com/386854/memories-sailed-away-marguerite/

56 **the TV Ingalls family:** Michael Landon (Pa), Karen Grassle (Ma), Melissa Sue Anderson (Mary), Melissa Gilbert (Laura), Sidney and Lindsay Greenbush (Carrie). *Little House on the Prairie,* NBC, 1974-1983.

56 **digging a furrow around their log cabin:** Laura Ingalls Wilder wrote of this event in Chapter 22: Prairie Fire in *Little House on the Prairie* (1935, Harper & Rowe)

58 **a break-off from the Missouri Synod:** As early as 1929, pastors belonging to the Missouri Synod felt that the Bible was clear on doctrine concerning the Antichrist, the millennium, and the conversion of the Jews but that these teachings were unsatisfactorily presented in the synod's Doctrinal Declaration. The Missouri Synod countered by stating the declaration is "not divisive" of church fellowship and went as far as saying that "it is neither necessary nor

possible to come to a perfect agreement in doctrine." This greatly troubled the orthodox pastors who believed in the inerrancy of the Bible, which they believed was written by holy men of God through God's inspiration and therefore was not open to interpretation. To worship with those who did not agree on the doctrine of God's word amounted to unionism and liberalism.

On Reformation Day, October 31, 1951, the Missouri Synod officially cut off support to a small group of pastors who would not sign the Doctrinal Declaration or church constitution. They and their families were evicted from their parsonages and, without a congregation to serve, left without a means of income. (The man who would become our pastor was one of these.)

Pastors from that initial break banded together in harmony for several years until a second break occurred when a pastor in their ranks was charged with unionism (for preaching to a congregation in the Wisconsin Synod). Most of the Minnesota congregations broke away at this time, leaving only a handful of pastors who decided to call themselves the Concordia Lutheran Conference (CLC).

From 1959 to 1980, the CLC dwindled down to five churches, one of which my family attended, and my grandparents helped secure in Seattle, Washington. The histories found on the CLC webpage–and which only document the history to 1980–do not detail the losses of individuals or families who either chose to leave or were excommunicated in these years and beyond. http://www.concordialutheranconf.com

60 **guest alpine, italian plum, italian plum:** My father said our alpine may have been the oldest tree in our backyard though it was the smallest. The tree was given to us by my mother's cousins who owned property in Cle Elum, and who

brought the tree to our family on a visit. The two Italian Plum trees were scavenged from an orchard that was cleared in south Seattle to make way for Interstate 5 in the mid '60s.

62 **REALM, DOMAIN (–of make believe):** The epigraph for this piece is a response from *Frontline: Currents of Fear*, Original Air Date: June 13, 1995 after the narrator asks: *But why would people fear power lines more than established risks, such as smoking and driving?* To which John E. Moulder, Professor and Director of Radiation Biology at the Medical College of Wisconsin replies: *People are less afraid of risks they think they control, and they're less afraid of risks that they understand, so the things that people are most afraid of are things they can't control and don't understand, and certainly power lines fall right in that category.*

62 **evidence of things not seen**: Now faith is the substance of things hoped for, the evidence of things not seen. (Hebrews 11:1 KJV)

63 **the Devil roams this earth:** Be sober, be vigilant; because your adversary the devil, as a roaring lion, walketh about, seeking whom he may devour. (1 Peter 5: 8 KJV)

64 **spiritually blind, dead, and an enemy of God**: The definition of original sin that we memorized from Luther's Small Catechism reads as follows: "Original sin (inherited sin) is the total corruption of our whole human nature. By nature, we are without true fear, love, and trust in God. We are without righteousness, inclined only to evil, and are spiritually blind, dead, and an enemy of God." *A Short Explanation of Dr. Martin Luther's Small Catechism, Handbook of Christian Doctrine*, (1943, Concordia Publishing House), p. 87.

74 **the No Tampon Tax petition:** Before 2015, the Canadian government considered all menstrual hygiene products a luxury, or non-essential item. This is no longer the case. As of this writing, the federal government of the United States still allows states to collect tax on menstruation products. www.canadianmenstruators.ca

78 **satanic rituals in basements and famous cemeteries:** It was said in the 1980s that Victoria, BC was the satan worshipping capital of the world. This rumor probably stemmed from publication of the autobiography *Michelle Remembers* (1980, Lawrence Pazder and Michelle Smith, Pocket Books) which documented satanic rituals and recovered memories that were easily discredited. https://nationalpost.com/news/canada/the-canadian-book-that-tricked-the-world-into-believing-they-were-overrun-with-satanist-murder-cults

83 **a formal letter via U.S. post**: Dear Katy, Inasmuch as you are a member of Saint– Lutheran Church, having been instructed and confirmed in the Christian faith, and having vowed in the presence of God and of this Christian congregation to be faithful to the Lord and His Word "even unto death," and to this end cheerfully to submit to the Christian discipline of this congregation as set forth in Matthew 18:15-17, we ask you kindly to meet with us as the voting members of Saint– Lutheran Church on Sunday, July 8th, at 3:00 in the afternoon to let each one of us express his own personal love for you and earnest concern for your soul. Perhaps one of us might be able, by God's grace, to bring something to you from God's Word, which, in years to come, may be invaluable for you personally. In a world filled with falsehood and deception, permit your brethren to talk to

you without malice or vindictiveness but straight from their hearts in all earnestness and sincerity. The people of this world are genuinely concerned about no one but themselves and about how they may use others for their own advantage. We are giving you an opportunity, in this letter, to talk with those who have nothing to gain personally and no advantage of their own to be concerned about but whose only concern in this meeting is to help you to be more aware of the way which you have chosen for yourself in this world and to urge you to return to your Savior rather than to be among those who "deny the Lord that bought them, and bring upon them swift destruction." (II Peter 2:1). Letter dated June 10, 1990, signed by the pastor and the secretary of Saint– Lutheran Church.

85 *Knots*: Though there are multiple books and articles written about and by R.D. Laing, I refer only to the following: *Knots* (1971, Pantheon Books) and *R.D. Laing: A Biography by Adrian Laing* (1994, Thunder's Mouth Press) and an article in The Guardian titled "My father, RD Laing: 'he solved other people's problems - but not his own'" first published on Saturday, May 31, 2008 in which R.D. Laing's son Adrian states: "When people ask me what it was like to be R.D. Laing's son, I tell them it was a crock of shit. It was ironic that my father became well-known as a family psychiatrist when, in the meantime, he had nothing to do with his own family." https://www.theguardian.com/books/2008/jun/01/mentalhealth.society

88 **the boy owns every self-help book**: I especially recall John Bradshaw's *Homecoming: Reclaiming and Healing Your Inner Child* (1990, Bantam); *On the Family: A New Way of Creating Solid Self-Esteem* (1985, Health Communications, Inc.) and, of course, Louise L. Hay's *You Can Heal Your Life*

(1984, Hay House).

90 **"Can't Get Enough of You Baby":** From Colourfield's 1985 album *Virgins and Philistines* recorded at Strawberry Studios, Stockport, England on the label Chrysalis.

101 **Love not the world:** John 2:15-17, KJV.

105 **the hammer is a myth:** The famous nailing of Luther's 95 Theses to the church door (which was commonly used as a public bulletin board) was first told by Philipp Melanchthon, a close friend to Martin Luther and a subsequent leader of the Reformation following Luther's death in 1546. However, Melanchthon was not in Wittenberg on the day he states he witnessed the nailing, and Luther himself never made mention of this incident in any of his copious personal or published writings. *Martin Luther: A Spiritual Biography*, Selderhuis, Herman, (Crossway Path, 2017) https://www.washingtonpost.com/news/retropolis/wp/2017/10/31/martin-luther-shook-the-world-500-years-ago-but-did-he-nail-anything-to-a-church-door/

107 **He fueled hatred of Jews and anabaptists:** When we studied Martin Luther's life in Bible Class, there was an underlying (and unstated) assumption that "*during the last decade of his life*, Luther emerges as a different figure–irascible, dogmatic, and insecure. His tone became strident and shrill, whether in comments about the Anabaptists, the pope, or the Jews." But the more I've read about Luther, the more I understand him as a life-long participant in the systematic racism and anti-Semitism of his time.
Martin Luther, the Bible, and the Jewish People: A Reader Paperback, Brooks Schramm (Author, Editor), Kirsi I. Stjerna

(Editor), (Fortress Press, 2012) https://www.britannica.com/biography/Martin-Luther/Later-years

Chapter Home

121 **the age-curled sign taped inside the display case**: I've recreated the wording of the sign taped inside the display case at the Deming Luna Membres Museum based on my memory and some research. Although many sources make these same main points regarding burial customs, we don't know for certain why bodies were buried in the place and position in which they were later found, and only the Mimbres know why they pierced holes in the bowls found placed over the faces of their dead.
www.pbs.org/wgbh/sisterwendy/works/mim.html
https://www.archaeology.org/issues/89-1305/features/738-mimbres-bowls-southwest-collapse-reorganization

124 **a black-and-white, twenty-three-pointed star:** Most of the information I found regarding the supernova of 1054 came from the 1990 *New York Times* article which states, "Painting on the bowl depicts a sunburst, believed to represent the explosion that created the giant glowing cloud of gas and dust known as the Crab Nebula, in the constellation Taurus." Star Explosion of 1054 CE Is Seen in Indian Bowl, by John Noble Wilford, *New York Times*, June 16, 1990.

126 **to let the devil out:** Archaeological evidence in Europe, Asia, and Mesoamerica suggest that trepanation—the drilling of a small hole into a person's skull—is one of our oldest human surgical procedures. Reasons for performing this procedure remain a mystery with theories ranging from trauma therapy,

initiations, or spiritual cleansing (as suggested in this piece). https://www.medicalnewstoday.com/articles/326281#Why-did-our-ancestors-do-it?

130 **"Cigarettes and Chocolate Milk":** From Rufus Wainright's 2001 album *Poses*.

136 **Rabbit became moon:** I found a version of the story of how the rabbit came to be on the moon in a Live Science post, which also talks about pareidolia, our tendency to create meaning from random sound and/or nebulous visual cues. https://www.livescience.com/34419-rabbit-in-moon-pareidolia.html

Gratitudes

Thank you to the home, land, and water that sustains me every day. The land where I live is the ancestral home of the Swift Water people who were forced off-island and onto the Puyallup Reservation in 1855. The trees of my island neighborhood are my eldest friends (by a few hundred years) and feel like family. I'm supported by their presence whether I'm aware of them or not. My house feels holy, surrounded as it is by water, but also because my husband, Greg, and daughter, Qwynn, live here with me. Their loving kindness and hair-trigger humor transform even the awfullest of days into a rich pleasure. Thank you.

I'm also grateful to many other humans who helped support the writing of this book: Susan Tower and Laura Thorne, early readers of the manuscript and sister-friends from way back (extra thanks to Laura for saying "Yes!" to letting Tolsun Books feature her painting *What Appears 2* on this book's cover). Heather Simeney MacLeod, brilliant friend and writer, who was my long-ago travelling partner and the one who once told me, "There are as many paths to God as there are people." Thank you to my writing group who stayed connected against all pandemic odds: Chris Balk, Michelle Bombardier, Suzanne Edison, Susan Landgraf, Susan Rich, Cindy Veach (and Elizabeth Austen, who read a few of these pieces in the beginning). Special thanks to the incredible Ann Teplick and our Third Place Books writing group from years ago, including Denise Calvetti, Esther Helfgott and Anne Hursey. And to Kelly Riggle Hower, teacher, poet, and a wonder of a human being.

I would like to acknowledge the Patterson family of Victoria, BC, who I never circled back to with my appreciation. Without their generosity and welcoming spirit, I would not have been able to move to Canada in the first place. Also, thank you to the friends I made and the people I met in Tofino, BC, who inspired me to protest and travel, and who helped me to see myself as a strong woman with a voice.

Thank you to the people who continually play a role in keeping me grounded in this life: Micha West and her children, Kepler and Geneva (who I love like they're my own); Stephanie Koura, who introduced me to The Colourfield in seventh grade; Jon, Janine, and Margot Lange who are always present; my dear Fox family: Allison, Patty, and Charlotte; John Overton, Alan Greenbaum, Rick Fabano; my New Moon Circle for the past fifteen years: Cecyl Fabano, Denise Rodriguez, Gretchen De Decker, Jamie Howes, Laura Lin, and Micha; and my Public Health-Seattle & King County friends and co-workers who keep holding the ship together through the pandemic's vicious storm.

Thank you to my entire family, especially my sister Trish who used to print and bind my high school poetry, and who taught me to appreciate office supplies as well as all the small, daily joys of life. To my incomparable Aunt Janet, and to my mom and dad, who did not close their door to me.

And finally, thank you to Artists Trust and the Centrum Residency in Port Townsend, Washington, where I began writing many of these pieces as essays. And to everyone at Tolsun Books (especially my kind and care-full editor, Percy Lind) you are an extraordinary group of people. Thank you for lighting the world with books!

Acknowledgements

"Crosses," "Northward Course," and "Good as Home": *Pithead Chapel,* Volume 7, Issue 7, 2018

"Pigeon Voyager": *Urban Animals Expeditions* (Dancing Girl Press, 2012)

"La Pincoya": *Till the Tide: An Anthology of Mermaid Poetry* (Sundress Publications, 2015)

"area of a partly machined surface left without machining" and "the people of a country: Sandra": longlisted for *PRISM International* Grouse Grind Super Short Fiction Contest, 2019 and 2020 respectively

"to touch at a place on shore" and "a portion of the earth's solid surface distinguishable by boundaries or ownership": read on Voice of Vashon 1650AM radio as part of *The Vashon Poetry Project*, Episode 1: Fall 2021

"September 12th": *Redheaded Stepchild*, Fall 2012

"Empty: Post–" and "Spiral: Pre–": *Pontoon Poetry*, Issue 13, 2017

"Empty: Post–": Pushcart Prize Nomination 2018

A variation of Chapter Home was published as *Night Watch*, winner of Floating Bridge Press 2017 Chapbook Contest

Katy E. Ellis grew up in Renton, Washington. Her chapbook *Night Watch* won the 2017 Floating Bridge Press chapbook contest. She is the author of two other chapbooks: *Urban Animal Expeditions* (Dancing Girl Press, 2012) and *Gravity* (Yellow Flag Press, 2014), which was nominated for a Pushcart Prize. She studied writing at the University of Victoria in British Columbia, Canada and at Western Washington University. Her poetry appears in a number of literary journals in Canada and the U.S. Her fiction has appeared in *Burnside Review* and won Third Place in the *Glimmer Train* super-short fiction contest. She has been awarded grants from the Elizabeth George Foundation, Seattle's Office of Arts & Culture and Artist Trust/Centrum. From 2014-2019, Katy co-curated WordsWest Literary series, a monthly literary event in West Seattle. She lives on Vashon Island.